Teaching Drama
in Primary and
Secondary Schools

University of
Chester

David Fulton Publishers
London

To Marianne

David Fulton Publishers Ltd
Ormond House, 26–27 Boswell Street, London WC1N 3JZ

www.fultonpublishers.co.uk

First published in Great Britain by David Fulton Publishers 2001

Note: The right of Michael Fleming to be identified as the author of this work has been asserted by him in accordance with the Copyright, Designs and Patents Act 1988.

Copyright © Michael Fleming 2001

British Library Cataloguing in Publication Data
A catalogue record for this book is available from the British Library

ISBN 1–85346–688–3

The publishers would like to thank John Cox for copy-editing and Sheila Harding for proofreading this book.

Typeset by FiSH Books, London
Printed in Great Britain by The Cromwell Press, Trowbridge, Wilts.

Contents

Acknowledgements

I am grateful to my wife Marianne who made many suggestions which improved the content and style of the text.

Several of the ideas in the book had their first airing in various journal articles. I am grateful to the editors and readers for their encouragement.

The English Magazine, Editor, Helen Hancock, vol. 1, no. 1, 1997; and vol. 2, no. 4, 1999.

Drama: The Journal of National Drama, Editor, Chris Lawrence, vol. 7 no. 1, 1999.

NJ (Drama Australia Journal), Editor, Christine Comans, vol. 23, no. 2, 1999.

Research in Drama Education, Editor, John Somers, vol. 5, no. 1, 2000.

Introduction

Aims

The aim of this book is to develop understanding of the theory and practice of teaching drama. It is not meant to be an introductory text but neither does it make too many assumptions about the reader's prior knowledge of drama and experience in teaching the subject. Its theoretical content derives as far as possible from real practical questions and likewise does not assume too much background knowledge in the relevant associated fields. The book as a whole is intended to provide a guide to, as well as a fresh perspective on, the recent history of drama teaching.

That history, as Bolton rightly stated in 1984, has been 'fraught' with 'rivalry' and 'polarity' (Bolton 1984:1). Writers and teachers have been divided over a number of issues but particularly the competing claims of 'theatre' (with its emphasis on acting, theatre skills and the performance of scripted plays) and 'drama' (with its emphasis on different forms of role taking, dramatic playing and improvisation). The difference of emphasis is described here very crudely. It is difficult to find the appropriate language with which to describe past divisions because concepts like 'theatre', 'acting', 'skills', and even the term 'drama' itself, have different resonances now, even after a relatively short period of time. It is only necessary to read Neelands on theatre, Bolton on acting and Hornbrook on skills (all 1998 publications) to realise the truth of that claim. The way language changes not only makes description difficult but can also be a source of confusion if the extent of the change is underestimated in writing about drama. It will be argued that superficial divisions (e.g. between advocates of 'theatre' and 'drama') have concealed deeper differences, which have more significance.

It was not uncommon for publications in the 1980s to declare that divisions were a thing of the past. 'Let's avoid stirring up old conflicts' was the title of a letter sent to *Drama Broadsheet* which called for a united front in the drama world and an end to 'bickering' (Davies 1985:13). Bolton declared his intention in his 1984 book to 'look beyond' the divisions and to sustain an 'eclectic view', and just five years later his own work came under strong criticism (Hornbrook 1989).

This custom for declaring an end to past divisions and heralding a new dawn of reconciliation has persisted in more recent years. In my first book on drama in 1994 I argued in favour of a 'balanced perspective' on drama teaching which among other aspects would recognise:

- drama as a subject and educational method;
- the value of a variety of approaches including performance and use of script;
- the different educational emphasis when pupils engage in performance;
- the importance of evolving criteria for evaluating drama.

In 1997 I went on to declare rather optimistically that the extreme divisions which were characteristic of the 1970s and 1980s had given way to a more inclusive view of the subject and that a consensus had been clearly established. I was not alone in my optimism. *The National Drama Secondary Teacher's Handbook* (National Drama Association 1998:i) also took the view that an 'inclusive' rather than 'exclusive' model of practice was now widely accepted. That publication was written by leading figures in the National Drama Association whose combined experience provided a more reliable reflection of the current state of affairs than my own more intuitive inference. Similarly Clark and Goode (1999:13) in their publication on assessment offer a more 'inclusive' definition of drama education which 'does justice to the range and diversity of activity undertaken by teachers and students of drama'. The definition of drama and theatre employed by Owens and Barber (1997:8) is 'intended to be inclusive'. Davies' Foreword to *Acting in Classroom Drama* states that Bolton (1998:ix) is 'at pains to find an approach that is inclusive'. Bowell and Heap (2001:1) also claim that 'the newly emerging consensus among drama practitioners recognises an inclusive model of drama within education'.

Two related questions come to mind in the light of these views. How widespread is the consensus alluded to here? What exactly does an 'inclusive' approach to the subject mean? Does it mean that any form of practice is acceptable? Does 'consensus' mean simply that there is a greater level of tolerance of different approaches rather than a coherent theoretical rationale or consistent set of practices? The consensus of tolerance and 'inclusion' may be widespread but that may not mean anything very significant. An inclusive approach might be interpreted as not so much a statement of a particular ideology but more a recognition that the vitriolic debates of the 1970s, 1980s and early 1990s have given way to a 'live and let live' approach where anything goes. In Britain, in the absence of separate subject identity in the National Curriculum, there is a greater level of autonomy than might otherwise have been the case. There is not total independence because the system of school and teacher training inspections maintains a fairly significant form of control. In the same way, although teachers can choose their own syllabuses and schemes of examination which reflect their own preferences, the choice has been much more limited in recent years. Despite these constraints, drama teachers do have more independence than teachers of other subjects so it is all the more important that their work is grounded in a coherent rationale.

An 'inclusive' approach to drama may mean simply that there is now greater tolerance of different approaches to the subject. While one department may place a major emphasis on traditional theatre and performing arts, in a neighbouring school the emphasis is very much on process work in which the idea of audience only emerges informally within the context of the drama workshop itself. Different practical approaches are likely to be driven by different aims. Research published by the NFER (Harland *et al.* 2000:499) found that a school judged to be high in 'personal and social outcomes' ranked lowest in 'knowledge of the art form' and pupils interviewed made little reference to technical skills in descriptions of their work. Another interpretation of an inclusive approach is that within a single department a variety of drama activities is embraced such as improvisation, mime, work on scripted plays, performance.

There is undoubtedly more harmony now than in previous years but some discordant notes have been sounded. Writing in 1999, Norman, who had been an influential figure in the field, returned to the drama teaching world after an absence of several years. He was not impressed by what he observed:

> After a time away from the world of Educational Drama, I recently participated in some conference workshops and observed some drama in schools. Nothing I experienced was inspirational, exploratory, owned, negotiated or characterised by participants working in the 'here and now' of drama, motivated by feeling engagement. It was largely mundane, sequential and cognitive, involving endless still images, exercises and an overwhelming concern with finding outer forms, most of which were deeply pedestrian.   (Norman 1999:8)

He goes on to 'wonder if this practice represents the brave new consensus of Drama Education' (ibid:8). The language Norman uses here is interesting. To the newcomer to drama his words may convey simply a qualitative judgement, a description of the ideal to which all teaching should aspire. However, the drama teacher who has lived through the recent history of the subject will recognise in the quotation a specific recommendation about practice. Central to his argument both here and in the rest of his article is the view that real 'feeling engagement' only happens through a certain type of practice which would always involve at least 'some element of whole-group drama and teacher in role' in order to provide 'high levels of arousal' (Norman 1999:12). The quotation also has some implicit philosophical assumptions, which will require more in-depth discussion. The overwhelming concern with 'outer forms' to which the quotation refers seems to imply an internal/external division, which will need closer analysis in subsequent chapters. Overall this is an unusually bold statement of what many would describe as traditional 'drama in education' beliefs. Here then is an implicit different version of recent history in drama teaching. What some writers see as 'consensus' and 'inclusion' may be interpreted by others as a concession to mediocrity and banality through an abandonment of all the positive developments that took place in the 1970s and 1980s when beliefs about drama teaching were held with passion and conviction.

Hornbrook has been very much associated with the challenge to those beliefs, and in his most recent edited collection reinforces his opposition to 'drama in education', criticising it for what he sees as its 'generalised aims and tenuous links with theatre' and describing it as a 'vagary of history rather than (as was once thought) an educational metamorphosis' (Hornbrook 1998:3).

Faced with these different views it is difficult to know how best to represent the development of drama teaching in the last 40 years or what stance to take at the present time. What is given here is a highly selective set of quotations and summaries which befits an introductory chapter but it is unlikely that even a highly detailed history would provide any view which is more conclusive. As often as some writers have fought for one particular stance, a similar number have declared that old arguments and old agendas no longer have relevance and should be put to one side. Such a view is not uncommon today. Some teachers and writers find that picking over the bones of old disputes is not always productive but that does not mean that tensions and differences can be ignored entirely and simply willed away. As Neelands (2000: 86) puts it, 'consensus can be a dead hand which stiffles necessary struggles within the field'. It is important, however, to know which issues are worth addressing even if they seem at times to be difficult to resolve. There is an argument for saying that to engage in any degree of seriousness with the business of teaching drama is inevitably to grapple with difficulties which seem unresolveable. To ignore them is to suffer from what Wittgenstein described as a 'loss of problems', a condition he ascribed to some philosophers. What happens then is that

> everything seems quite simple to them, no deep problems seem to exist any more, the world becomes broad and flat and loses all depth, and what they write becomes immeasurably shallow and trivial.
>
> (quoted in Sluga and Stern (eds.) 1996:6).

This quotation seems very relevant to policy makers in education in general at the present time. Simple and instant solutions are preferred to any deep exploration of issues: national testing of highly dubious validity has replaced the professional sharing of judgements which belonged to a more formative system; target setting, punitive inspections, the prescribed methods of the literacy hour are all part of an obsession with certainty. Ironically while much of academic writing in the past 15 years has been dominated by postmodern notions of contingency and uncertainty, many educators in their professional lives live in a world which has become 'broad and flat'.

Wittgenstein's choice of the word 'broad' here is typically interesting and challenging for the term usually has positive rather than negative connotations. After all, is not one of the explicit purposes of the National Curriculum to offer pupils a broad experience? What I take Wittgenstein to mean here is the tendency to oversimplify, brought about by a failure to slow down, to pause and focus on particular issues in some depth. It was part of his method to examine problems from a variety of different perspectives and different directions, making connections, thinking of examples, inventing metaphors and asking probing questions. It is that 'dwelling within' which is missing from much contemporary discourse in education. The need for a curriculum to have breadth tends to be taken for granted at the present time but might there not be an argument for suggesting that 'depth' might be more desirable than 'breadth' and that the two are not always compatible. The concept of 'depth' will be explored more fully in Chapter 6.

Structure

If, as stated, the aim of this book is to develop understanding of the theory and practice of drama then the method will be to elucidate and explore some of the tensions and difficulties which arise and which can help in examining differences. It is for that reason that the chapters are structured around pairs of concepts which are often seen in partial opposition to each other or even as polar opposites.

In planning the organisation of this book I was faced with a dilemma of creating a *structure* which would be useful but at the same would not place too many limits on the reader's *experience* of the text. Organising the book around concepts does place some limitations because that structure does not allow separate treatment of particular themes such as the recent history of drama teaching. The advantage, however, is that particular themes can be examined in a variety of different contexts in order to gain a fresh perspective. Because the different concepts are constructs and bear no precise, simple relationship to reality, there will be an inevitable overlap between them not just horizontally but vertically as well. In other words 'content' can be explored not just in relation to 'form' but also in relation to 'experience' and 'means'. The concept of 'understanding' can usefully be characterised as 'making connections' and in this context the connections work in different directions. The connections between the pairs is shown in the following list:

content ——— form
experience ——— structure
means ——— ends

internal	———	external experiences
making	———	responding
feeling	———	form
process	———	product
meaning	———	logic
expression	———	representation

Another reason for adopting this structure is that so many theoretical and philosophical issues throughout history can be conceived in terms of binary concepts: appearance and reality (pre-Socratic), mind and body (Descartes), fact and value (Hume), natural necessity and practical freedom (Schiller). Dewey took the view that all philosophical problems derive from dualistic oppositions. Challenges to dualistic ways of thinking have come from Hegel (his notion of synthesis through dialectical thinking) as well as from more recent postmodern writers. The connections, which the book seeks to make therefore, are both internal within drama as well as external to other intellectual disciplines and traditions.

The discussion of drama aims to connect with wider issues in education, art, aesthetics and philosophy as well as with wider social concerns. For example, we live at a time in which, in almost every aspect of public life, surface appearance is given precedence over underlying reality. This is true of the preoccupation politicians have with 'spin', of education policy makers' adherence to cosmetic rather than deep improvement in standards, and the tendency for punitive inspection regimes to conceal rather than uncover truth. Connections can be made between the issue of content and form in aesthetics with popular notions of style and substance, surface appearance and reality. Similarly, the tension between structure and experience is relevant to many of the assumptions underlying the National Curriculum and new literacy strategies but also links to intellectual debates surrounding structuralism and poststructuralism in literary theory.

Practice

The structure of the book therefore is intended to address some of the questions, which arise as an inevitable result of engaging seriously with drama as a subject. This is not a matter of raking over old problems but rather of seeking to avoid inhabiting an oversimplified world which is broad and flat. Centring the discussion on pairs of concepts will facilitate the connection with theory. However, theoretical discussion can all too easily descend into abstruse and self-justifying obfuscation. Each pair of concepts therefore is in turn related to a specific practical issue so that the importance of relationship between theory and practice is kept to the fore:

Learning in drama	——	content and form
Planning lessons	——	experience and structure
Planning schemes of work	——	means and ends
Assessing drama	——	internal and external experiences
Progression in drama	——	making and responding
Working with script	——	feeling and form
Performing drama	——	process and product
Drama and language	——	meaning and logic
Drama and aesthetics	——	expression and representation

A common thread through several of the chapters will be the theme of language, not just through an exploration of the relevant concepts and connections but by considering the implications of views about language and meaning. Wittgenstein (1953:109) described philosophy as a 'battle against the bewitchment of our intelligence by means of language'. Philosophical problems are solved not by seeking new information but by rearranging what we already know and being aware of the way language can confuse thinking. That does not mean that he viewed philosophy as something rarefied and irrelevant. 'What', he asked, 'is the use of studying philosophy if all that it does for you is to enable you to talk with some plausibility about some abstruse questions of logic, etc. and if it does not improve your thinking about the important questions of life?' (Monk 1991:424). Theoretical discussions about drama similarly need to illuminate and improve thinking about practice. Practical questions related to such issues as planning syllabuses, formulating objectives and developing teaching methodology can sometimes be informed from unlikely theoretical sources.

Faced with any pair of polarised concepts and attendant problems, it is tempting to conclude that the theoretical and practical solution lies in recommending a balance between the two extremes, with the danger that what is being recommended each time is something of a bland compromise. Such a conclusion is invariably too much of a simplification. One reason is simply that recommending a balance is in effect to say nothing of very much significance. Even if the concept of finding a balance between two extreme positions is accepted, the key question has to be what such a balance looks like in practice. A deeper problem, however, is that simply to recommend a balance implies that the polar positions are in fact real ones, that the pairs of words do in fact signify separate entities in the world. In almost every sphere of intellectual debate we have to face the inadequacy of language which carves the world up too simply. The use of the term 'integration' is intended to suggest the idea of conceptual fusion rather than 'balance' which rather implies trying to find the appropriate midway point on a continuum. It is also preferred to 'synthesis' because this term implies a blending, and loss in separate identity of the separate substances.

Integration

Having adopted the concept of 'integration' as a central unifying theme in this book I had several misgivings about using it. First of all it has a different, more common, meaning in education to the one intended here because it usually refers to the practice of linking subjects with another when planning and teaching the curriculum. The concept of an integrated curriculum gained ground in the 1970s but has largely been ignored in Britain since the advent of the National Curriculum. In other countries the idea has retained more prominence. My intention in using the term is not primarily to recommend the integration of drama with other subjects or with other art forms although both issues are worthy of debate in their own right.

Another danger of coining the idea of an 'integrated' approach to teaching of drama is that it may appear that what is being recommended or attempted is a new 'grand theory' of drama. This is far from being the case. It will become apparent through the book that the term 'integration' is not being used to describe a new form of practice but is being adopted as a construct to seek to inform and clarify theoretical and practical aspects of teaching drama. Many writers and teachers adopt what I would describe as an 'integrated' approach to the subject and I will draw from the work of others to illustrate the idea. The introduction of a new word is simply to throw a 'fresh seed on the ground of the discussion', not to advance a new theory (Wittgenstein 1998:4).

The use of the term 'integration' has both a practical and theoretical import. It is intended to signal that the concept of an inclusive approach to teaching drama is not in itself enough if the term merely signals acceptance of any approach without discrimination. The notion of inclusion in drama is in danger of conceding too much ground to those writers who see little value in the major developments in drama in education that took place in the 1970s and 1980s. While the intention is not to turn the clock back or to wallow in nostalgia, it is important that the new generation of drama teachers understand the important advances as well as mistakes which were made at that time and the ways in which they can inform contemporary theory and practice.

Drama in education

Where can the legacy of drama in education be found in contemporary practice? That is not an easy question to answer. The origins of the use of 'conventions' which dominates much current practice (using still image, questioning in role, thought tracking, etc.) can be traced back to Heathcote and Bolton who are generally acknowledged as the leading exponents of drama in education. Norman on the other hand did not find in the endless still images and exercises which he observed anything resembling the quality of engagement he had been used to. For him whole-group improvisation lead by teacher in role provides the context for the most successful drama. It is then not always easy to discern or articulate what the legacy of drama in education is, for it is more frequently defined in terms of what it is *not* rather than what it is – as 'something other than theatre skills, improvisation, role play or performance' (Peter 1994:5).

Drama in education is usually defined as a particular type of practice. This is the approach taken by O'Toole (1992:3) who defines drama in education as 'fictional role-taking and improvisation'; O'Neill (1995) who prefers the term 'process drama'; and Bolton (1998) who describes 'making' (which embraces 'living through' drama) as a particular category of acting behaviour. Some writers equate 'living through' with 'process' drama; others do not. These categories will be explored in subsequent chapters. Taylor (2000:1) writing very much from a drama in education tradition defines drama praxis as 'the manipulation of theatreform (*sic*) by educational leaders to help participants act, reflect and transform'. What all of these writers share is an implicit assumption that drama in education practice involves a particular set of practices which usually involved a highly skilled teacher leading a group through a series of rich artistic and educational experiences relying heavily on different kinds of improvised work. However, by reducing drama in education to one particular set of limited practices in this way there is a danger of conceding too much curriculum ground. If the legacy of 'drama in education' is confined to one set of practices it is unlikely to inform important debates about progression, skills acquisition, responding to drama, performance and assessment.

One of the themes of this book will be to explore an alternative view, to examine whether it is in fact more helpful to see the legacy of drama in education as a fundamental way of looking at the teaching of drama rather than a particular set of practices. What that means in theory and practice will be explored in the rest of the book.

The book aims to link theory and practice but it does not have as many examples of practical lessons and suggestions as some other publications. It is intended to complement other works rather than duplicate their content. Primary and secondary teachers of the subject who are interested *primarily* in practical suggestions (examples of games, exercises and drama structures) would do better to look at some of the many useful texts now on the market to which reference will be made throughout this book. However, I have met very few drama teachers who are not interested in theoretical questions related to their subject. For four years in the 1990s I was privileged to act as external examiner to the outstanding MA drama courses run at the University of Warwick (by Jonathan Neelands and Joe Winston) and at the University of Central England (by David Davis and Tag McEntegart). That rich experience reinforced my view that drama teachers from all over the world share a passion for theoretical ideas when they serve to illuminate practice. The same view has also been confirmed by teachers with whom I have been fortunate to work with in recent years. I have benefited particularly from discussions with Tony Gears (Egglescliffe School), Sue Garside (Grangefield School) and Jill Scrimshaw (University of Durham). Previous research scholars at the University of Durham have helped broaden my perspective on drama; I am particularly indebted in this respect to Tadeusz Lewicki of the Pontifical Salesian University in Rome. Current research students at Durham (in particular Yoon-Jeong Choi and Chih-hui Lai) have also helped to give me an international perspective and to see the teaching of drama through fresh eyes. I refer to the teaching and writings of Gavin Bolton and Dorothy Heathcote many times in the book and their work has been a considerable influence. It would also be disingenuous not to acknowledge that David Hornbrook has had an affect on my thinking, just as he has on many others writers on the teaching of drama in the last 12 years.

CHAPTER 1

Learning in drama: content and form

Introduction

Two different drama lessons are being taught in two neighbouring schools. In the first the teacher has given the pupils a group task to work out how they might represent through dialogue and movement the landing of a spacecraft on an alien planet. Towards the end of the lesson the pupils demonstrate their ideas and each group's performance is subject to critical comment by the teacher and class. In the second school, during an improvisation of an imaginary press conference set in the future, four pupils in role as space travellers are being questioned about the civilisation they encountered on another planet.

One way of characterising these two approaches is to say that one is placing more emphasis on form, the other on content. Whereas the first lesson is more focused on technical questions associated with representation, the second lesson is rather more concerned with the theme. The focus of the learning in each lesson also seems to be different; in the first case the emphasis is more on developing technical skills in contrast to the second lesson which on the face of it seems to have more potential for exploring ideas. The two cases are given here as examples rather than to imply any qualitative judgement about these lesson extracts taken here out of context. To make any significant judgement it would be necessary to evaluate not just a single lesson but the project as a whole. The first lesson might lay the foundation for the devising of a drama which poses significant questions about human life and nature through a fictional journey to another planet. The second lesson may continue in a way which makes a rather more elaborate use of dramatic form.

The concepts of 'content' and 'form' have been convenient ways for some writers of characterising different approaches to drama teaching. Daldry, in his forward to Hornbrook's (1998) edited collection *On The Subject of Drama*, claimed that 'too much drama work with young people privileges content over form'. In the last 30 years drama lessons have focused on social concerns like homelessness, bullying, child abuse but 'what we see more rarely, however, is an exploration of theatre forms' (ibid: ix). Along with an undue emphasis on content he suggests there has been a preoccupation with a 'semi-improvised naturalism' as the 'dominant mode of expression'. Daldry is making a criticism here about the predominance of one style of drama which might have had some truth in the 1970s but is no longer the case; even a brief skim of any recent book would show the wide range of varied approaches which are now part of the drama teacher's repertoire (Nicholson 2000, Bennathan 2000). His criticism, however, does raise questions about whether content or form should have priority in defining learning objectives in drama. A prior question, however, is to ask what is meant by the term 'form'.

Uses of 'form'

In writing about drama the concept of form is used in different ways with different types of emphasis reflecting the varied use of the term through the history of art theory, e.g. 'balanced structure' (Aristotle), 'harmony leading to perception of essential being' (Aquinas), 'metaphysical structure of reality' (Plato), 'design' (Kant) (Hanfling 1992:144). For the purpose of this discussion I propose to describe five different uses of the term in the context of drama. It is important to stress that this is not an attempt at systematic categorisation but rather a description of language in use. This is an important distinction because a presentation of categories implies a listing of discrete types which can be easily distinguished from each other. The five uses of 'form' (described here by using the terms 'essential', 'genre', 'style', 'cultural' and 'individual') overlap to a considerable degree and are often subsumed one within the other which makes the use of the concept all the more confusing.

   The word 'form' is sometimes used to refer to some general notion of the defining characteristics of art itself, what might be termed 'essential' form. In some ways this is a poor choice of term because the dangers of essentialism in ascribing meaning to language is a central underlying theme of this book. However, it does highlight one important defining characteristic of art. According to Schopenhauer the art form 'plucks the object of its contemplation from the stream of the world's course and holds it isolated before us' (quoted in Hanfling 1992:146). The Russian formalists saw the process of art or literature as one of 'making strange' or 'defamiliarising' the familiar (Shklovsky 1988 (first published 1965)), a similar concept emerging in the work of Brecht with more social and political purpose. Expressing a similar sentiment, if somewhat more obscurely, Sartre (1972) refers to the work of art as an 'unreality'. What these views have in common is that art relies essentially on human intervention and intention which is what distinguishes the notion of 'art' from the 'aesthetic'. We can be moved aesthetically by a sunset but we reserve the term 'art' for products made by an artist. This idea is captured well by Dewey (1934:48):

Suppose for the sake of illustration that a finely wrought object, one whose texture and proportions are highly pleasing in perception, has been believed to be a product of some primitive people. Then there is discovered evidence that proves it to be an accidental natural product. As an external thing, it is now precisely what it was before. Yet at once it ceases to be a work of art, and becomes a natural 'curiosity'. It now belongs in a museum of natural history, not in a museum of art.

This insight can be related to drama by means of an example. Imagine that a drama lesson is taking place in a school classroom. In the 'play' a 'normal' lesson is taking place with the teacher and pupils assuming the roles of teacher and pupils: as yet nothing particularly out of the ordinary is happening during the fictitious lesson. If anyone walked in from outside they would be hard pressed to know that what is going on is not in fact just a lesson. It would not be unreasonable to say that there is little use of form (in one sense of the term) in the lesson. But form is involved in the broadest abstract sense because all participants are accepting the overarching convention that the situation is not real.

Peter Handke's play *Offending the Audience* (Handke 1997) explicitly challenges all the normal conventions of the theatre. As one of the speakers (not characters) says:

> These boards don't signify a world. They are part of the world. These boards exist for us to stand on. The world is no different from yours. You are no longer eavesdroppers. You are the subject matter. The focus is on you. You are in the cross fire of our words.... We are not conducting an exhibition purely for the benefit of your enlightenment. We need no artifice to enlighten you. We need no tricks. We don't have to be theatrically effective. We have no entrances. We have no exits, we don't talk to you in asides.

Yet there is, as Kuhn (ibid:x) puts it in the Introduction, a 'glorious paradox' in that the piece which takes a stance against the normal conventions of theatre is being presented inside the theatre and cannot escape its one, overriding essential defining characteristic.

The term 'genre form' has been adapted from Eldridge (1992) to refer to general defining aspects of drama, as distinct for example from other art forms such as visual art, music or the novel. O'Toole (1992:3) uses the term 'genre' to describe different manifestations of drama practice (of which drama in education is one) and points out that the use of the term has become complicated by genre theory. Bolton and Heathcote (1999) refer to different types of role play genres. The intention here is to describe rather than prescribe different characteristic uses. Reflection on how drama as a genre itself is different, say from poetry or the novel, can illuminate practice. Drama operates through the use of space, time, tension, focus and symbol but other arts employ these aspects of form as well. Listening to a concert takes time as does contemplating a painting. Sculpture occupies space; a novel often relies on creating tension, and poetry uses symbol. It is more helpful to explore how drama employs these and other aspects of form in *distinctive* ways.

Examples of genre form in relation to drama:

- meaning is largely conveyed through dialogue

In as much as drama penetrates the internal world of its characters, it does so through external dialogue rather than through discursive description of inner states as in the novel. This is important because pupils need to acquire the skill of exposition without the luxury of using prose description for scene setting. Overuse of a technique like thought tracking or narration is contrary to drama as genre because one of its essential aspects is to convey hidden meanings and sub-texts through surface dialogue and action.

- time can be manipulated but also constrains

When a drama is in the process of being devised it is possible to intervene and freeze time (although this facility does not extend to the performance of a play as a product). It can accelerate or slow down time (as in the case of the novel) but it gives the illusion of occupying 'real time' (unlike the novel). A play takes a defined amount of time (2 to 3 hours) irrespective of the time span covered in the fictional context.

- it operates in the immediate present

The fact that drama operates in the immediate present (not in a recorded past as with film) is one of its distinctive aspects. It is important for teachers to recognise that live drama is different from film and television drama. It cannot be subject to editing in the same way. It relies in performance on the presence of a live audience to whom the actors react and relate. It is therefore a more communal experience than film or television.

- it relies on focus

Visual art also relies on focus. The importance of focus in drama, however, is that it selects and foregrounds particular elements for attention while giving the illusion of replicating real life. The fact that in drama participants can create the appearance of reality (because they are real people, occupying real space and time) knowing in fact that their actions are free from real consequences is one source of its educational power. So much has been written against the use of naturalism in drama teaching that it is tending to appear less and less in the drama classroom (in favour of such techniques as tableaux, stylised repetition, thought tracking, etc.). However, Styan (1981:1) has rightly pointed out that what counts as 'naturalistic' changes over time. He quotes Edward Craig who observed in *On the Art of the*

Theatre that each development in acting seemed more 'natural' than what came before.

> In time Antoine made Irving look artificial, and in turn Antoine's acting 'became mere artifice by the side of the acting of Stanislavski'. What then, asked Craig, did it mean to be 'natural'? He answered, 'I find them one and all to be mere examples of a new artificiality – the artificiality of naturalism.

Styan suggests the same thing is true of writing plays. The depiction of a breakfast scene or of a family watching television if it is to count as 'good' drama, is unlikely to be *entirely* naturalistic because it is unlikely to reflect reality in a simple way (see Chapter 9).

These descriptions of form have to be seen as a *characteristic* rather than *necessary* aspects of the artistic medium in question. For example a novel may be written purely in dialogue, just as a monologue or soliloquy in drama appears to depart from the more normal dialogic form. Shakespeare used soliloquy to convey inner thoughts while Greek drama used the chorus as commentary on the action. These examples do not deny the value of identifying aspects of genre form but indicate exceptions to the rule will be found. Drama evolves and changes over time: it is always trying to 'find ways of breaking out of the temporal and spatial restrictions of its medium'. (Styan 1981:1).

The term 'form' is also sometimes used to describe what might be termed different dramatic 'styles' (e.g. realism, symbolism, expressionism, epic theatre), also sometimes called 'genres'. 'Style' has been described by Styan (1981:xii) as 'the way of seeing of writer, player or spectator' and the '*sine qua non* of dramatic communication'. Although different styles tend to be associated with different playwrights they are often interwoven:

> Ibsen is a realist and a symbolist, Strindberg embraces both naturalism and expressionism, in writing a symbolist drama Pirondello becomes a progenitor of the absurd...
>   (ibid:xii)

Style may influence the way we describe genre (providing further evidence of the complexity of the use of the terms). Among the characteristics which Styan lists as being associated with the early expressionist play he includes the following: 'the plot and structure tended to be disjointed... instead of the dramatic conflict of the well-made play, the emphasis was on a sequence of dramatic statements... the dialogue, unlike conversation was poetical, febrile, rhapsodic...' These characteristics might provide a different description of genre form than if we had a more conventional 'naturalistic' play in mind. Such considerations show how fluid these concepts are.

The term 'form' is also used to refer to different approaches across 'cultures' as in theatre forms (kabuki, noh). Brachmachari in Hornbrook (1998) points out possibilities of investigating the particularities of peoples, histories and artistic practices through drama. She argues that giving pupils experience of theatre from different countries (particularly non-western traditions) is likely to promote values of tolerance, sensitivity and understanding as well as widening pupils' predominant conception of drama as pure naturalism. This is not to advocate a study of other forms of theatre simply as that of an exotic 'other' but 'as a means of exploring the exchanges which have, and are, taking place between peoples of different cultures and histories'.

The term 'individual' has been used to refer to those aspects of form which distinguish one piece of work from another (specific use of movement, lighting, sound, symbol). Eldridge (1992:159) describes individual form as follows:

> When...we are struck by the distinctiveness of a particular work and by how any alteration in it would ruin its particular sense and effect, then we are tempted to say that an artistic form is just what is proper to any particular work.

In an educational context individual form can also refer to specific conventions within a drama (freeze frame, questioning in role).

To summarise then, the term 'form' is used in the context of drama in varied ways. These uses are not definitive categories for they overlap and relate in complex ways. 'Focus' for example can be seen as an example of essential form (because all art selects or brackets off from the current of real life), of genre form (because this selection and bracketing happens in a particular way) and individual form (the aesthetic impact of a particular drama often relies on a specific type of focus). The descriptions are not definitive. For example one might want to add that the concept has been used in the past in a prescriptive sense as when Aristotle elucidated the concept of tragedy in terms of specific formal characteristics or in a more abstract sense as when Langer (1953) defined form as 'an articulation'. Form is often used in writing about drama teaching to refer to structure (which will be addressed in Chapter 2). The five uses identified here, however, will serve the purpose of exploring the concept of form in relation to teaching and learning of drama.

When Daldry argues that school drama has not emphasised form he may be correct only in the sense that schools have not used theatre forms from different cultures or a range of styles. It might well be argued that a drama curriculum which provides superficial knowledge of a range of different cultural and style forms may run the risk of inhibiting rather than promoting deep understanding of genre form.

Much of the educational value of drama derives from its 'essential' form, from the way it functions as an art form in the broadest sense. Its value lies not so much in replicating real life (an assumption which many pupils through the influence of television bring to their work) but in exploring experience in ways which cannot happen in real life. This insight is important when considering the type of drama which is appropriate for young children. In the early years of primary school the work more resembles children's dramatic playing. It would be a mistake to introduce types of individual form prematurely in order for the work to qualify in some sense as art. The source of learning is likely to be found more in the 'essential' form.

Technical knowledge about drama is often conceived in terms of individual form but this sometimes results in a rather low level of objective. It is easy to see why this is so from the analysis given here. Individual form is embedded in a particular drama and therefore is difficult to abstract as a skill divorced from context. Many attempts to describe skills in drama in relation to conventions seem rather lame precisely for that reason. One of the assumptions of drama in education practice was that with a skilful teacher outstanding drama could be produced with a group, irrespective of their skill or experience. This is one extreme position. But the opposite view is to make the mistake of elevating practices which come fairly naturally to pupils to the status of a skill to be specifically taught. Harland *et al.* (2000) describe 'improvisation' as a technical skill but most pupils who are old enough to hold a conversation find improvisation easy *provided they have something to say*. Most groups can be taught how to create a tableau within minutes; ability in drama resides not in practising the abstracted skill of tableau but in creating a tableau which embodies significant meaning. It is the relation of individual form to content which is important.

Unity of content and form

One of the problems when discussing the relative claims of content and form is that they are not always easy to distinguish. The unity of content and form or 'matter' and 'substance' has been a long held tenet in thinking about art. It derives partly from the idea that meaning in art is unique and not able to be paraphrased or translated: 'It is impossible for a work of art to say or to show what it does in any other form without significant loss of content' (Graham 1997:50). Another associated idea is that 'content' and 'form' cannot be separated from each other: 'the only true works of art are those whose content and form prove to be completely identical' (Hegel quoted in Szondi 1987:4). This in turn leads to the notion that attempts to explain the meaning of a work of art are bound to be unsuccessful. 'The art created is the meaning; it does not have to be extricated to serve propositional knowledge' (Abbs 1992:5). Kaelin (1989:12) expresses the idea as follows:

> Content and form . . . are not antithetical terms; as if the artist first possessed the form and then poured the content of his own experiences into it as a mould giving form to those experiences – or as if the artist first possessed the content to be expressed before discovering a form fitting for its expression. Both these approaches seem to be in error.

Acceptance of the principle of the unity of content and form can reinforce the belief that form should take precedence over content when planning, teaching and assessing drama, not because content should be ignored but because it is thought that it can take care of itself. Drama after all is always about something; content is always present. In the 1970s and 1980s writers on drama in education struggled to articulate the type of learning which pupils derived from drama in relation to content. Propositions of the kind which claimed that pupils changed their attitude from a 'policeman is the enemy' to 'a policeman is a man with a home and family' were difficult to substantiate and therefore difficult to use as a means of assessing drama. Form, however, provides a more tangible assessment objective and there have been precedents in the history of thinking in art for privileging form over content.

Significant form

The theory of 'significant form' in aesthetics is an extreme version of this view because it does not just leave content to take care of itself but actually denies its importance at all: to appreciate a work of art we need bring with us nothing from life, no knowledge of its ideas and affairs, no familiarity with its emotions' (Bell 1969:91). This view may seem somewhat eccentric now but it is best understood in a historical context. Bell's notion of significant form can be seen as a challenge to simplistic ideas about representation which saw the purpose of art as representing reality as closely as possible. As Collinson (1992:144) has pointed out, Bell's theory applies more to the visual arts and 'was written at a time when the work of Impressionist and Post-Impressionist painters was a source of perplexity to many people'. They could see little merit in the new styles of painting because they had been used to judging paintings by reference to their content and subject matter rather than to their formal aspects.

The degree to which form or content is emphasised in the context of making and responding to art can partly be judged then in a historical context, in terms of a corrective response to what came before. This is also true of teaching drama. In much of the improvised drama of the 1970s content was given a high profile. This was evident in the notion of 'drama for learning' or 'drama for understanding' because the object of the learning implied by those statements was very much concerned with content, with learning about life and particularly about relationships and social issues (this idea will be discussed in more detail later in this chapter). It is important, however, to guard against any tendency to simply reverse the emphasis purely as a reaction against what came before (as happened in the case of theories of significant form). This would place undue emphasis on form (or a particular category of form) at the expense of content.

If we return to the examples given at the start of this chapter it will be apparent that the first lesson does seem to diminish the importance of content. It was suggested that a judgement about this lesson can only be made in the light of knowledge of how the project as a whole might develop. That is true but if the example given here of pupils practising landing a spacecraft is characteristic of the work as a whole the technical aspects are being pursued at the expense of any significant content. There is content of some kind in that the drama is about a journey to another planet but it does not appear to be of any significance. In the drama there is undue emphasis on representation (on getting it to look right) with insufficient recognition of the implications of 'essential' form (in what ways does the framing of this particular action illuminate life experiences?). Here there is a significant difference between visual art and drama. In the context of the former, advocates of a theory of significant form were challenging the adherence to notions of representation in judging art. In drama an excessive emphasis on representation can in fact lead to an undue preoccupation with form at the expense of content.

Significant content

Despite arguments in aesthetics about the indivisibility of form and content, it does sometimes appear that it is possible to translate or convey the meaning of a particular piece of art by a statement of its content. We might want to say that the simple statement 'I love you' conveys the content of Auden's *Lullaby* which begins,

> 'Lay your sleeping head my love ...
> Human on my faithless arm
> Time and fever burns away
> Individual beauty from
> Thoughtful children ... '

Lyas (1997:99) suggests that someone making the simple statement 'I love you' may be using words which are as full of feeling as any written by a poet. However, he goes on to argue that although the poem may not differ from a humbler expresssion in intensity, it does so in range. 'There is more language in the poem, and so the range of reverberations, resonances and associations of the words will be immeasureably greater'. The poem is not just a statement of love but a statement among other things about the transitory nature of experience. The whole poem has a lyrical feel but the inclusion of the word 'faithless' in the second line undermines any possibilities of over-romanticism. It is possible to abstract content from form in some way but meaning is lost in the process.

Compare this to the treatment of 'I love you' in a drama workshop described by Hahlo and Reynolds (2000:144). The scene is fairly simple: three friends share a house and are having breakfast together – their talk must centre on breakfast. The improvisation is allowed to proceed until one of the participants is told secretly by the teacher that she is in love with one of the house mates. They can still only talk about breakfast.

The improvisation will change. Ask the observers to comment on what they see. Before they say, 'Louise fancies Martin', they may also say that Louise has been told 'to do everything for Martin', or that she is trying 'to freeze out Natalie'. All of this information comes from giving one of the performers a strong objective: 'I want to tell you I love you'. Ask the spectators to say which was the more engaging of the two improvisations to watch, and they will invariably say the second. The objective gives the scene structure and the spectators are drawn in. They may not necessarily know what the objective is; it is just more interesting to watch someone in pursuit of something.   (ibid:145)

For this exercise to work the pupils who are performing need some understanding of the notion of constraint which can be interpreted as an important element of genre form. An inexperienced group may not understand the necessity for constraint even though this is built into the structure of the scene – the girl in question may come in and simply sit on the boy's knee thus destroying any element of subtlety in the exchange. The form works more through depth than extending range (as in the poetry example). That is not to say that the Auden poem does not have depth but the drama does not add on allusions and references but places an extra layer of meaning below the surface of what is happening. Form adds depth to the content but that does not stop us being able to abstract content from form in some way.

Before considering the importance of the relationship between content and form to the concept of learning the discussion will be extended in depth as well as range by detailed examples.

Lesson examples

The following text was used as a stimulus for a piece of experimental drama which will be examined in terms of the content and form of the work produced. Two groups of pupils of different ages and experience were given the same stimulus (four lines of verse) and asked to devise a piece of drama. This was not intended to be a normal drama lesson; the intention was to observe and record how pupils set about the task of devising a drama without any help from a teacher. The verse used to intitiate the drama was taken from the final scene of Brecht's *Gallileo* (although it is worth pointing out that not all versions of the play contain this final scene).

One, two, three, four, five, six
Old Marina is a witch.
At night, on a broomstick she sits
And on the church steeple she spits.

Before reporting on the way in which the different groups of pupils set about their task it is worth examining the verse in terms of it own content and form. It has no significant narrative content or tension and any dramatic potential is not immediately obvious. It takes the form of what appears to be a child's rhyme although, perhaps because this is a translation, the rhythm and rhyme are somewhat discordant; there is a uniform six syllables in the first and second lines but the flow of these lines is not rhythmical because the staccato beat of line one gives way to a more ruptured beat with a one and then three syllable word starting line two. Someone engaged in a traditional practical criticism of the text might seek to relate the fractured verse to the flight of the witch on her broomstick but we could equally claim that it is simply the result of poor translation. It is, however, worth musing over the content and structure of the lines because this is what determined the pupils' response, however unconsciously.

The two groups of seven pupils (age 16 and 11) were both told that this was an experiment rather than an ordinary lesson. Both groups were told that they might find the task challenging, there were no real limits on time and both gave permission for the work to be video recorded. Their instruction was that they would be given a few lines of written text and that they should try to create a piece of drama based upon them. The text could be incorporated into the drama but that was not a requirement; it could if they chose be read alongside it. Once the text was handed over there was no more discussion with the teacher until the work was finished.

The seven Year 12 pupils (who happened to be all girls) were part of a theatre studies group and had considerable experience of drama (including GCSE) and knowledge of drama conventions. They were clearly used to devising work in small groups and set about the task with confidence. They focused very much on the text itself and started off by considering ways of representing each line using tableau and thought tracking. They experimented with different readings and accompanying actions. The first product was simple but accomplished as far as it went: six of the pupils as young children gathered in a circle and each shouted a number from the first two lines; the seventh pupil as Marina appeared on the outside and circled them as she uttered the second line. The 'children' then voiced their ideas about Marina: 'She's got a cat', 'She's got a broom as well. I saw her last night', 'And a cauldron' etc. The third line from the poem was incorporated into the conversation as the final individual utterance 'at night on a broomstick she sits' with all of them joining in for the last line.

This first 'product' amounted to more of a dramatised reading than a piece of drama *per se*. The pupils were using the content of the verse to determine the drama in as much as their presentation was about a witch but it was the form of the verse which had a greater determining factor in the way the work was constructed. I suspect that had the pupils been given the brief to construct a drama about a witch they would, given their experience, have produced something with more emphasis on meaning and content. Although it had not been part of the original instruction they were somewhat limited by the form of the verse and felt compelled to use it and replicate it in their finished product.

The work might well have finished there had not one of the pupils suggested that what they had represented might in fact be just what was 'in the children's minds'. It was then that the work started to develop and acquire more significant content. They now took the view they had no need to represent a witch in the drama and the main focus centred on the one young child, Tammy, who insisted that Marina was just an ordinary old woman. They included extra scenes in which the group of children and Tammy reacted differently to Marina; the 'outsider' child being drawn to the outsider 'witch'. The second product started and ended with the rhyme, but in the final version the children substituted the words 'Old Marina' with 'Little Tammy', the one child who had stood out from the others (she was also physically outside the circle). The second product was more satisfying as drama because its content was more significant. Although it still appeared on the surface to be about a witch, it focused at a deeper level on peer pressure and non-conformity. The second version did not discard the formal elements which they had worked on in the first attempt; the ritualistic and rhythmical chanting of the rhyme, the use of the circle to symbolise the boundaries between the insiders and outsider, the use of disembodied voices to externalise thoughts all contributed to the second version.

The Year 7 mixed ability pupils (three boys and four girls) had little prior experience of drama. Two had participated in extracurricula productions but overall their experience of school drama was limited. They were extremely well motivated and applied themselves to the same task with enthusiasm and considerable imagination. Their initial suggestions were wide ranging and focused predictably on the possible content of the drama: 'it could be set in ancient times and everyone would be thinking she's a witch', 'they don't know she's a witch', 'there is a house in the background with all these kids walking by saying nasty songs and pointing', 'one, two three, four, five, six could be bells on the church at night', 'it's the time she's about to come out', 'the children echo it and on six she turns into a witch' etc. However the pupils were not easily able to translate these ideas into dramatic form. Their first product was a classic piece of dramatic playing; pupils took it in turns to be the witch and chased the others who ran away screaming in excitement. The playing had its own charm and shape but, because the pupils could not find an appropriate form, it lacked any significant content.

In order to find an appropriate form in which to embody and develop their ideas, it was necessary for the teacher to intervene and help them. This part of the project was planned in order not to leave them with a sense of failure at the end of the work but it also provided another example of the relationship between content and form in a concrete context. As it happened the pupils did not feel that their 'play' had failed but they welcomed help in developing their ideas. The nature of the intervention consisted in some focused questioning which was designed to probe their idea that the rhyme turned Marina into a witch. This had featured in their original discussion but had been lost in the attempt to bring the ideas to life. The pupils also needed help in selecting specific scenes in order to convert the narrative into a plot. Their second product had more narrative content. Marina was an old woman who had helped when a young child had become injured in the park. Marina's gossip in the neighbourhood (criticising the parents and exaggerating her own efforts) turned the community against her and rumours spread that she was a witch. The local antagonism and teasing (children knocking on her door and running away) resulted in her actually turning into a witch (enacted at the end in very stylised way).

The pupils supplied these ideas but they needed assistance in using three different defined spaces and some help in constructing different scenes and the use of a 'whispers' convention to simulate the spread of gossip.

Both groups produced work which initially lacked meaningful content; the Year 12 pupils sought to represent the verse using their knowledge of dramatic form, the Year 7 pupils engaged in dramatic playing. The older pupils used their initial formulation and their broader understanding of drama to develop the work further. The teacher's intervention with the Year 7 pupils indicated the kind of skills the pupils could in time be taught to use independently (ability to structure drama into scenes, finding beginnings and endings, seeing ways of approaching the text obliquely). In both cases the themes emerged in a social context from inside the construction of the drama. The creative process was one in which the emphasis was on the making of the drama rather than any prior emphasis on significant meaning; the latter was rather 'discovered' in the process. The learning and understanding with regard to content emerged through the process of group articulation and expression. In both examples meaningful content emerged through handling of form but it was by no means a necessary consequence. The Year 7 pupils had created a simple narrative which derived its depth from its metaphorical content (a person's behaviour and personality is often a result of the way they are treated) which had certain resemblance to a folk-tale or myth. This content was not planned and worked out in advance but emerged from the engagement with the form: finding a simple focus to convey ordinary life in an economical way, symbolising the spread of gossip, enacting the transformation and so on. An element of rather exaggerated 'theatricality' also contributed to the final product. One of the pupils was more confident than the others as a result of her previous experience in school productions and she needed no help in acting out the transformation in a very physical way. That confidence was less productive in some of the earlier scenes in which her determination to *act* ran the risk of detracting from keeping a focus on the central theme.

Learning in drama

In order to use the terms 'content' and 'form' productively we have to accept the principle of indivisibility discussed earlier, the view that in the context of art, meaning is a function of both content and form. That does not mean, however, that we cannot use the terms freely to identify different aspects of drama. In fact not to do so runs the risk of a dangerous form of reductivism whereby either one important component is ignored or else it is assumed that reference to one concept automatically includes the other. To acknowledge that form and content are indivisible, but in practice they are going to be referred to separately, is not an eccentric use of language but the way all language functions (a view which will be developed in Chapter 8).

To what degree is it desirable to make reference to content when planning lessons and describing the outcomes of drama? Advocates of drama in education saw in the formulation 'drama for learning' a way of embodying the change of attitude or understanding which came about as a result of participation in the drama and which transcended mere developmental objectives or acquisition of personal qualities. In other words the notion of 'drama for learning' focused attention very much on the content of the drama rather than on the form. Bolton's early attempt to describe learning in drama in propositional terms (e.g. pupils learn that 'a policeman is a man with a home and family') was abandoned in favour of a description of the more general mental powers which promote understanding (Bolton 1979, 1984).

The problems with describing learning in propositional terms at first seem fairly clear. It seems to suggest that the specific learning accrues in a single lesson or project (for how can pupils continue their learning if the topic has changed?). If the objectives of the drama are to help pupils learn that 'a policeman is a man with a home and family' we are entitled to ask, 'did not pupils know this before the drama started?' Even if we manage to find a means of assessing this kind of knowledge (which seems unlikely) how do we determine that it has been acquired as a result of the drama? It has been argued by some writers that isolating the learning in this way in propositions seems to be a betrayal of the art form because the content is embodied uniquely in the art form; separation of form and content in this way is not appropriate.

These objections, however, are only valid if the propositional learning in question is seen in the same way as a fact or piece of information, e.g. 'that candlelight was used to light the stage in the early nineteenth century'. Both have the same external form but they fulfil different functions. Again it may be useful to borrow a term from Wittgenstein to suggest that the two types of propositions actually belong in different 'language games'. Languages and language games can only be properly understood in particular contexts and not in isolation from the functions they serve. Language is 'part of an activity' (Wittgenstein 1953:23) and can only be understood within particular forms of activity. With that view it is easier to see that a claim to learning with reference to content in drama is not the same as learning a piece of information and should not be subject to the same rules and expectations.

The classic challenge to the claim that drama has brought about a particular piece of learning is to ask 'how do you know?' and that question has either drawn a blank or set some writers off in search of proof. But when Keats claimed, using a propositional form, that 'Beauty is truth' he was not asked 'how do you know?' (Greger 1969). That question in the context of drama only becomes valid if the claim to learning is being used as the object of assessment. It will be argued in Chapter 4 that descriptions of pupil progression and accounts of assessment need to be undertaken in terms of pupils' developing knowledge and skills related specifically to drama rather than the learning and understanding related to content. However, that does not mean that the importance of content should be undervalued in the context of planning and teaching drama.

There is value in specifying the content, theme or understanding (even expressed in propositions) which is relevant to particular drama projects, as long as it is recognised which 'language game' is operating when such terms are used. Some drama in education practice may have been guilty of overemphasising content at the expense of form. It is important to ensure that significant content is not lost or seen as irrelevant in the quest for formulating objectives which can be assessed. To try to isolate content from form in conceptual terms is not necessarily to impoverish meaning. The total import or meaning of a work of art may be ultimately elusive but that does not mean that it cannot be unpacked in discursive terms (Greger 1969). We can discuss the meaning of a play but transferring this talk to a different 'language game' can bring ludicrous results. If someone claims that by watching *King Lear* they learned 'that life can be cruel' it would be crass to object that they must have known this already.

The content of drama can be described in a highly reductive way which conveys no real sense of significant meaning (e.g. *King Lear* is about 'families'). It may be useful therefore to coin the term 'significant content' (to adapt a term from the aesthetic formalists) to go beyond a simple statement of theme. Drama, according to Heathcote depicts matters of 'significance' (Johnson and O'Neill 1984). The theme of a drama may simply be described as 'bullying' but its significant content needs to be conveyed in rather different terms, e.g. 'exploration of the complexity of a bully's character'.

This is far from being the end of the discussion of content and form. As indicated in the Introduction to this book, the different concepts cannot be examined in isolation from each other and the implications of the discussion here will be explored further in subsequent chapters. As suggested, one way of conceptualising the relationship between content and form is to see form providing shape or structure to content which is rooted in experience. The tension between structure and experience therefore needs further consideration.

CHAPTER 2

Planning lessons: structure and experience

Chapter 1 described a lesson with a group of 11 year olds based on a short extract from Brecht's play *Galilleo*. The lesson outlined below represents one attempt to translate that same project into a drama structure to be repeated with other classes. The idea of a 'lesson outline' is used here to provide a shorthand summary of the key stages in a lesson, its structure, as opposed to a lesson plan which would give more details of objectives and context.

Lesson outline

1. The teacher places the verse on a board and asks the class to read it aloud; the pupils are told that they are going to create a play based on this extract.
2. In small groups of three/four, pupils are told to devise a scene set in a park in which Marina helps a young child who has had an accident but then insults the boy's parents when she takes him to his home.
3. The teacher assembles the pupils in a circle, introduces them to the 'whispers' convention and they go round the circle repeating rumours about Marina, each tale becoming more exaggerated than the one before.
4. Using mime, each group acts out a scene in which the local children tease Marina by knocking on her door and running away.
5. The pupils enact, in a stylised way, Marina's transformation into a witch culminating in a still image with Marina in the centre of a circle surrounded by the children.

I suspect that many teachers of the subject will realise that there is something not quite right about that lesson outline. It has been based on a drama which worked well with one group of pupils but the attempt to create a lesson which can successfully be repeated is not easy. One general problem is that different groups respond differently to the same stimulus or tasks but that is true of any lesson plan. What is it about this particular structure which makes it problematic? In the case of the original lesson the teacher was building on the pupils' own ideas, helping them find a form in which to articulate and develop them. In the example above the teacher has a highly directive role which is in danger of removing from the pupils any proper sense of ownership. Without any real commitment to the drama (to the content or the chosen form), the pupils may either be bored and disengaged or unable to apply themselves to the work with any level of seriousness. An alternative method would be simply to provide the pupils with the verse as stimulus and ask them to devise a drama of their own choosing. The problem here however is that it leaves rather too much to chance and leaves the precise role of the teacher and the objectives of the teaching extremely vague.

The challenge of gaining real commitment to the drama is one of the reasons why work on text was neglected in many drama classrooms. The contrast between the intense personal experiences accessible through spontaneous improvisation and what was seen as the more objective, sterile work on plays written by others meant the latter was studied as literary text in the English classroom rather than brought to life in the drama workshop. This view will be explored in more detail in Chapter 6.

An alternative approach to structuring the lesson on the Brecht extract will be described later in this chapter but even with the sequence of five activities given here, a more productive start might be to introduce the whispers convention in the form of a game right at the beginning. This would provide a more appropriate introduction and at least allow the teacher to focus the class on one aspect of the significant content: that gossip in a community can cause damage. However, other activities still rely too much on telling the pupils both what to do and how to interpret the stimulus material, rather than giving them scope to make their own connections.

The challenge identified here can be described as a tension between 'structure' and 'experience'. The advantage of working with predetermined structures is that it is easier to identify significant content, learning outcomes, appropriate dramatic forms and assessment opportunities. The danger however is that it is all too easy to pay insufficient attention to the quality and nature of the experience of the participants in the drama. This tension is not unique to drama although it is more pertinent to an artistic endeavour in which the quality of feeling involved is of particular significance. The polarity between structure and experience represents in microcosm a much broader set of contrasting approaches to curriculum planning. The conflict between traditional and progressive education has dominated a great deal of debate in education. According to Dewey, writing some 65 years ago, 'the history of educational theory is marked by opposition between the idea that education is development from within and that it is formation from without' (Dewey 1938:17). More recently and somewhat more obscurely the contrast has emerged as a distinction between 'modern' and 'postmodern' approaches to curriculum planning.

Theoretical background

Almost 60 years after Dewey, Doll (1993) made a similar set of polarities central to his book, *A Postmodern Perspective on Curriculum*. The modernist paradigm is seen by him as a closed, linear, easily quantifiable system in contrast to a postmodern approach which is more complex, pluralistic and unpredictable. The following quotations from the Foreword to the book (ibid:x) capture the flavour of the positions which are identified:

Open-endedness is an essential feature of the post-modern framework

Mind is not a passive mirroring of nature, but the human ability to actively interpret and transform concepts in ways that make lived experiences meaningful and useful.

an open system will allow students and their teachers in conversation and dialogue to create more complex orders and structures of subject matter and ideas than is possible in the closed curriculum structures of today.

Doll offers his own vision of a curriculum utopia 'where no one owns the truth and everyone has the right to be understood', where the teacher is a leader, but only as an equal member of a community of learners. Metaphors will be more useful than logic in generating dialogue in this community. There also will be a new conception of educative purpose, planning, and evaluation that is open-ended, flexible, and focused on process not product.

Readers who are familiar with drama in education as it developed in the 1970s might be having a strong sense of déjà vu reading these extracts. There is more than an echo of early Heathcote, Bolton and other exponents of drama in education with the emphasis on negotiation of meaning, process and flexibility. Doll's aim 'to make a conscious attempt to redefine curriculum not in terms of content or materials (a 'course to be run'), but in terms of process – a process of development, dialogue, inquiry, transformation' is strongly reminiscent of early writing in drama in education (ibid:13). Open-endedness, flexibility, handing over responsibility to the pupils were central tenets of its practice. The following quotation is fairly typical of writing at the time.

Dorothy Heathcote is not out to cleanse *experience* of its bewildering variety or mystery. She reminds us that the information available at any given moment is neither neat or linear – it comes at us in a swirl of images and sensory data. In this chaos Heathcote discerns *structure* and pattern, but always the structure is subject to transformation in the next moment. She relishes the possibilities available in any particular situation and thrives in the dynamics of subtle changes in relationship.   (Wagner 1976:166) (*My italics*)

This belief in an open, flexible attitude to lesson planning was epitomised in drama by the practice of starting every lesson with the question to the class 'what do you want to do a play about?'. This radical approach was in contrast to classrooms in other subjects where often pupils would be found writing silently or listening passively to teacher exposition. It is little wonder that many progressive teachers embraced the open approach with enthusiasm but found it difficult to operate it successfully from day to day in the classroom. Lessons which seemed so easy when they were demonstrated by 'master practitioners' often ended up with pupils hiding under rostrum boxes or running around the drama classroom. It would have been small comfort to those frazzled teachers to know that they were operating in a postmodern paradigm.

The contrasting paradigms identified by Doll are derived not just from educational theory but from a wider view of the history of Western thought, including different accounts of knowledge and truth. He identifies three 'metaparadigms': pre-modern, modern and post-modern. Pre-modern thinking (from recorded Western history to the scientific and industrial revolutions of the seventeenth and eighteenth centuries) was characterised by a sense of natural order, of harmony and balance.

> Along with balance the Greek concept of order also had a strong sense of closure and stasis. Boundaries were finite, immutable. To step over boundaries, out of one's destined position or class, was to court the fates and in mythology to risk the anger of the Gods... Ptolemaic astronomy and cosmology, building on Euclid, also envisioned the universe as closed and circular.   (Doll 1993:24)

Modernism developed with the rise of scientific thought and the attempt to control nature by determining its laws. It was predicated on a notion of a stable, uniform universe whose laws could be discovered. Postmodernism on the other hand is according to Doll characterised by acceptance of lack of stability. The belief that certainty was attainable through 'right reason' gives way to a more open vision predicated not on positivistic certainty but on pragmatic doubt, 'the doubt that comes from any decision based not on metanarrative themas (sic) but on human experience and local history' (ibid: 61).

Doll is not alone in educational literature in extolling the importance of 'human experience' over 'positivistic certainty' and yet, as stated in the Introduction to this book, there is a great contrast between the theoretical ideas in academic writing and a preoccupation in current policy and practice with rigid, mechanical systems and different forms of sterile clarity. The chasm between theory and practice can be attributed in part to the fact that these positions are occupied too rigidly as alternative choices, rather being seen for what they are as enabling constructs or metaphors. There is also a difficulty for writers in knowing quite how to apply to education the radical philosophical conclusions associated with postmodern thinking so that either there is retreat into common sense pragmatism or an acceptance of some rather bizarre conclusions.

What, for example, are the educational conclusions to be drawn from ideas such as these: 'there is no such thing as objective truth', 'everything is culturally contingent', 'truth is not discovered but made', 'the traditional distinction between fact and fiction does not hold', 'description and interpretation are no longer viable', 'there is no reality structured independently from human thought'? The modern version of these ideas echoes the humanism of William James who declared in 1907 that our truths are 'man-made products' and that 'man engenders truths upon a malleable world'. These sentiments are quoted by Cooper (1998:38) who goes on to comment on the degree to which such thoughts have become commonplace on the educational scene. He identifies the ways in which they have surfaced:

> They include: enthusiasm among many maths and science teachers for a 'human', 'constructivist' mathematics and science; 'death of the author' or 'role of the reader' doctrines with their denial of 'pre-existent' text, possessing a determinate meaning, there to be encountered; 'conventionalist' and other 'non-cognitivist' conceptions of moral judgement; and the image of historical writing as a form of 'fiction'.

If there is no distinction between fact and fiction there is little point in having pupils do anything but tell imaginative stories in history lessons. If as teachers we cannot allow ourselves to say that something is true how do we give any real meaning to the concept of teaching? Different forms of 'radical constructivism' have been influential in many areas of education in recent years. These ideas have been less directly influential in drama (although not entirely absent) but the legacy of progressivism can be found in the elevation of the significance of the participants' experience over and above any concern with an external body of truths (for none such exists) or in the reluctance to deal in objective knowledge (for knowledge is always constructed). Drama teaching has through much of its history certainly resisted any attempt to initiate participants into a form of knowledge. Taylor's summary of positions held by Hornbrook and Heathcote are not that distant from the polarities under discussion.

> Hornbrook's idea of an effective drama class is one which 'must restore the dramatic product to a central position'. When Heathcote aims to collaborate with her students, Hornbrook ensures that teachers 'must ensure that (they) are taught what they need to make progress' (1991, p.22). Hornbrook demands 'attainment targets' in drama, whereas Heathcote appeals for 'authentic experiences'. Hornbrook finds such descriptions mystifying ((1989), 1998, p.18). In his role as an arts inspector, he argued that 'a knowledge-based

curriculum' which addresses the 'inspectors' concerns over purpose and progression' is required (1998, p.15). When Heathcote speaks of negotiating the curriculum, Hornbrook proposes 'a field of knowledge, understanding and skills which constitute drama as a discipline' (1991, p.21). Both seem to have a different perception of praxis, of how a curriculum should be constructed.

(Taylor 2000:106)

It is tempting to look for a resolution of such differences by determining the 'correct' philosophical position. Unfortunately life is not that simple. One pole of the philosophical argument rejects any notion of objective truth. The consequent retreat into subjectivity and relativism therefore does not allow the advancement of a position which can make any claim to 'correctness': advocates of that position are inevitably hoist on their own paradox. More seriously, the attempt to apply philosophical insights directly to educational practice in this way is in danger of moving unwittingly from one language game to another.

Cooper (1998:47) makes the important point that the kind of remarks which arise from what he calls the 'hermeneutical-cum-constructivist position' are 'not intended to ruffle the surface level of ordinary practice and discourse where the familiar distinctions...do their work'. They are, he suggests, 'strategic remarks in campaigns against other and older philosophical positions'. It is a mistake to apply the philosophical arguments from one 'language game' directly to the practical business of living, including teaching, where common sense distinctions can operate in peace (contrary to what many educational theorists have argued). According to Wittgenstein we are drawn into philosophical confusion because language bewitches us. Doubting the existence of normal everyday objects has no real meaning in our day to day life.

> I am sitting with a philosopher in the garden; he says again and again, 'I know that that's a tree', pointing to a tree that is near us. Someone else arrives and hears this, and I tell him: 'This fellow isn't insane. We are only doing philosophy.'   (Wittgenstein 1969:467)

Doubts about whether we can ever claim to know anything are not helpful if applied directly and naively to the business of teaching. However we do not have to jettison such ideas completely as being irrelevant to practice. If such philosophical insights are seen not so much as simple statements about reality but as statements which draw attention to the way language has meaning, their relevance is more apparent. The focus on language prevents us lurching from an extreme form of subjectivity to a rigid commitment to objectivity. Rorty (1989:3), writing in the tradition of Wittgenstein and Davison, claims that truth is 'made' rather than 'found' but he intends this more as a statement about language than about the way in which we gain knowledge of the world. It is not for example an insight which is designed to persuade scientists that they are wasting their time because they might just as well invent the truth.

> We need to make a distinction between the claim that the world is out there and the claim that truth is out there. To say that the world is out there, that it is not our creation, is to say, with common sense, that most things in space and time are the effects of causes which do not include human mental states. To say that truth is not out there is simply so say that where there are no sentences there is no truth, that sentences are elements of human languages, and that human languages are human creations.   (ibid:4)

This notion of the contingency of language will be a central theme in Chapter 8 but in this discussion of structure and experience it does allow an escape from the impassse between blind adherence to one or other of the polar concepts. It is language itself which points not just to the integration of the competing positions but also to the integration of theory and practice.

A 'soft' form of postmodernism does not argue that scientists merely discover truth in the sense that they can go out and make up anything they like. Nor does it regard science or any claim to truth in education as nothing more than a 'narration', myth or social construction. Postmodernists who draw on science to embrace such ideas make themselves vulnerable to the type of hoax orchestrated by Sokal and Bricmont (1998:199) who exposed the emptiness of this position. Sokal's spoof article accepted for publication in an academic journal used bogus science to argue, among other things, that it is false dogma to claim 'that there exists an external world, whose properties are independent of any human being and indeed of humanity as a whole'. The 'soft' position acknowledges that we are given access to truth and knowledge largely through language which derives its meaning from shared social and cultural contexts.

If we take the implicit view that language gains meaning simply by being attached to objects or events in the 'external' world this will lead to a blind adherence to objective structures and a blind adherence in the classroom to 'pressing on regardless'. If on the other hand it is believed that language gains its meaning inwardly by its simple correspondence with thoughts this will lead to undue emphasis on subjective experience.

Practical implications

It is by a consideration of the way in which language can be said to have meaning that polarities associated with subjectivity and objectivity can be reconciled. One implication of this discussion is that the search for methods of integrating structure and experience in the classroom has a stronger theoretical basis than the mere sharing of practical ideas. Theoretical discussion alone in the context of education does not take us very far without an exploration of practice; Doll's analysis of different paradigms does not give much indication of what a 'postmodern' approach to constructing a curriculum might look like in practice except a sense of harking back to old, fairly vacuous ideas associated with extreme forms of progressivism. On the other hand, the sharing of practical ideas for teaching without some framework of pedagogical principles derived from theory only informs planning in a superficial way.

The rest of this chapter will explore some of the practical implications of seeking to integrate 'structure' and 'experience'. A distinction needs to be made between structuring a piece of drama and structuring a lesson, although understanding of one can help to inform the other. In process drama the teacher often plans the lesson by working out how the structure of the drama will unfold. However, structuring a *lesson* might involve deciding at what stage responsibility for structuring the *drama* is handed over to the pupils. Often in the past these alternatives have been conceived too starkly; either the teacher took sole responsibility or handed it over completely to the pupils. Understanding such techniques as 'framing' the pupils in relation to the content, engaging their attention, creating atmosphere, injecting layers of meaning (all derived from drama in education practice) can inform lesson planning.

The tendency towards polar positions in the theoretical literature is also found in drama publications which have a practical orientation. At one extreme are the breezy 'ideas for drama lessons' books which are direct, uncomplicated, 'thin' and highly structured. These books capture more the spirit of the educational times, certainly in the UK, where there is an increasing popular assumption that education is a simple and straightforward business. At the other extreme are books containing lessons perceived not as simple formulae but more detailed, thick descriptions of complex procedures which are very context specific. Both types of books have their limitations in terms of helping teachers develop their practice because the lesson ideas are too directive and unsubtle in one case or too extravagant and individual in the other. However, both types of books can be very useful if their content is viewed in terms of generalised pedagogic principles which underlie and inform practice. Many of the techniques which are familiar from the drama literature, can be employed with more purpose and in more varied ways if seen as methods of integrating structure and experience.

Bolton (1998:222) has described a dramatic sequence based on Arthur Miller's *The Crucible* which contains a very interesting rationale for all the techniques used and choices made in the project. The opening activity is simple and effective. The pupils are asked to make a rapid list of all the superstitions they can think of. This kind of brainstorming activity is a useful start to a drama lesson because it gives pupils some ownership, gets them active from the start, invites them to make some investment in the topic in a non-threatening way and provides a focus for discussion and ideas. The activity is developed in a subtle manner by Bolton. He asks each of the group to put their initials by the superstitions they are affected by. Those few pupils who have not signed to any of the superstitions are momentarily isolated and excluded from the group in a light-hearted way, thereby introducing the class to one of the themes of the play.

Owens and Barber (1997:46) describe a drama sequence based on the theme of a travelling fair which was introduced by asking the pupils to stand in a circle and try to think of 40 rides or stalls that can be found in the fair. Again this is an effective and deceptively simple start; it contains an element of tension (can we reach the target?), injects pace and energy, unites the whole group in a common goal, hooks them into the chosen topic, and uses their ideas which can feed into the next activities. O'Neill (1995:105) used teacher in role as a talk show host to introduce the theme of 'famous people'. She asked each person in turn to say, in one sentence, the best thing about being famous. When they have made their contributions a question is posed which deepens their thinking and lays the foundation for the development of the drama in the lesson. With a class of seven year olds Winston (2000:17) describes the use of physical activity (creeping as if through a wood and freezing in silence) to introduce a drama about a stranger living in a clearing near a village. Bennathan (2000:131) describes an activity which was used to introduce a drama on 'rites of passage' to Year 9 pupils (13 to 14 year olds). They are asked to share sentiments which begin with the phrase 'When I was your age...' which have been expressed to them by adults in the past. In pairs they then create short scenes showing an incident in which they have not been treated as grown up. They are limited to a small number of lines of dialogue. This simple introduction leads to complex and challenging drama activities.

These are just some examples of the way experienced practitioners limit the tyranny of an imposed structure without losing any sense of pupil ownership, direction and purpose in the lesson. If we return to the Marina lesson, how could the structure have been altered to be less directive? One method might have been through the introductory activity. Allowing the pupils some time to read the text and brainstorm possible interpretations and possibilities for drama would serve to increase their initial involvement. If the intention is to press on with the pre-planned structure, regardless, then the brainstorming activity can appear to be no more than a piece of subtle manipulation whereby the teacher chooses selectively from the suggestions. However, the activity does not have to be undertaken in that manipulative way if the teacher is open about the purpose of the initial sharing of ideas. The brainstorming and discussion can provide a bridge between the pupils' own ideas and the focus of the lesson, in Dewey's terms it provides an 'organic connection between education and personal experience' (Dewey 1938:25).

The inclusion of an initial brainstorming might not be enough to hand over sufficient challenge and ownership to the pupils. In order to achieve that objective the task at stage 2 could be presented differently. Instead of asking the pupils to show the scene in the park they are asked to prepare and act out the events which turned the village against Marina. An alternative lesson outline is given below.

Lesson outline

1. The teacher informs the class that the text will be used as the focus for the lesson. The verse is distributed and pupils are asked to read it in their groups and to brainstorm questions about Marina which arise from reading the verse.
2. The groups share their thoughts and in the course of the discussion the teacher poses the question: 'Suppose Marina is not in fact a witch. Why do the children chant this verse?'
3. The teacher assembles the pupils in a circle, introduces them to the 'whispers' convention and they go round the circle repeating rumours about Marina, each tale becoming more exaggerated than the one before.
4. In small groups the pupils are asked to prepare and act out the original scene which caused the community to turn against Marina. This is the main part of the lesson.
5. The scenes are shared and analysed in terms of content (was it a trivial incident or a misunderstanding? were the people justified in their reaction? etc.) and in terms of the effectiveness of the dramatic presentation.

This lesson outline is an improvement on the first. There is an element of artificiality in the way the content has to be introduced but there is a strong structure which provides security for teacher and pupils. It should be stressed that the account here is included not as an example of a model lesson but to illustrate the difficulties of creating the necessary fusion of elements. In the lesson described in Chapter 1 the whole concept of Marina's transformation came originally from the pupils; the problem with both examples here is that they are seeking to build the same idea into a preordained structure which is quite a challenge.

It was suggested earlier that the whispers 'game' or 'exercise' might provide an appropriate introduction to the Marina lesson. There are many reasons for using warm up games and exercise but if they are being used explicitly to integrate structure and experience they need to be chosen carefully so that they do lead into the specific theme of the lesson. This is important with regard to other activities. Care needs to be taken that pupils are not being asked to invest large amounts of time in devising ideas which have no real bearing on the subsequent work, for example when pupils are asked to invest considerable energy in such activities as drawing, creating a tableau or devising rituals which do not contribute sufficiently to the overall purpose of the lesson.

Consider the brief summary of a lesson structure given below.

1. The class are divided up into two groups as two rival gangs. They are given various tasks to deepen commitment to the work:
   – invent the rules for the gang
   – draw a plan of the headquarters
   – invent a password.
2. The pupils are given instruction and various pairs exercises in how to mime a fight which they enact in a stylised and controlled way.
3. The pupils are placed in role as members of a community given the task of solving the youth problem in their town, each with a different vested interest in the outcome. The teacher adopts the role of chair and is able to stimulate and prompt the different factions.

This outline corresponds fairly closely to a lesson structure which I employed in my early teaching career which can now be viewed more critically on the basis of the theoretical discussion in this chapter. All the activities are in themselves valuable but the pupils spend a considerable amount of time investing in the creation of gang identity which does not integrate with the main part of the lesson. There is a worthy attempt to inject significant content into the drama but this takes place in the context of a discussion in roles which is more akin to an English speaking and listening exercise.

In contrast, a lesson described by Winston and Tandy (1998:42), which was planned for five to six year olds, manages to balance a tight structure with techniques to engage the pupils while having overall a clear sense of purpose. It is not possible to do justice to the lesson here; readers are referred to the more detailed description in Winston and Tandy's *Beginning Drama 4–11* which contains further advice and issues to consider. Instead I will highlight those aspects which are particularly relevant to the theme of this chapter.

- The children sit in a circle and the teacher spreads out a quilt and pillow with a teddy in the 'bed'. (This 'theatrical' start hooks the children in and without too much fuss they are invited to give names to the teddy and the child who owns it, drawing them in further.)
- Teacher in role as child answers the children's questions and includes the information that the teddy wakes up when she is asleep. (The teacher can convey essential information in this section of the lesson which also gives responsibility to the pupils because they have to take the initiative.)
- The pupils take on the roles of other toys which come alive at night. When the teacher in role wakes up the children freeze, replicating a popular game. (The children choose which toy to be so they have individual responsibility and their own personal investment within the structure.)
- The teacher now takes the role of the teddy and shares concerns with the other

toys that the child is unhappy at school. (The significant content has now been introduced and the lesson develops with inbuilt controls; for example, the children have to whisper in case they wake up the child, but they are given freedom to find solutions to the boy's problem.)

Teaching structure

It is apparent from the literature that the predominant current approach to planning in drama is what might be termed a 'conventions' approach (using hot-seating, tableaux, role on the wall, thought tracking, improvisation) in different combinations. This method is helpful particularly to newcomers because it places structure at the forefront of the planning process. But the 'conventions approach' does have its drawbacks, particularly if used in the wrong way. In the wrong hands it can offer a fragmented experience to pupils and narrow the range of the drama curriculum. For example the underlying implicit assumption is often that it is the teacher rather than the pupils who is responsible for structuring the drama. When Nicholson (1994) argued that drama teaching is more than the 'familiar' drama structures of still images, hot-seating and sustaining roles this brought a spirited defence of this approach to planning because it was questioning an approach which was highly valued by many teachers (Ackroyd 1995).

The key point then is not to question the conventions approach *per se* but to recognise the dangers. It can easily place undue emphasis on structure at the expense of quality of experience or deny pupils themselves sufficient control over the structure of the drama. Schemes of work can become highly routinised with lesson one consisting of pairs work, still image, teacher in role, group meeting; lesson two consisting of teacher in role, group meeting, still image, thought tracking. This 'perm any four from five' method of planning can become as bland and predictable as any other type of teaching. It is easy to see why this approach has been embraced by teachers because in an educational climate which places a premium on control and accountability, the preplanned sequence provides an element of certainty. However, used in the wrong way and experienced as a sequence of episodic events the approach can deprive pupils of a real sense of unity in the drama which is created.

It was suggested in Chapter 1 that often conventions are translated into drama skills in schemes of work and that this is problematic because the skill itself (thought tracking, tableau) is not in itself hard to acquire. What is sometimes missing is a recognition of the need for pupils themselves to learn how to structure drama as an aspect of genre form. The lesson plan given below designed for 12 to 13 year old pupils is based on an idea in *The Art of Drama Teaching* (Fleming 1997b).

Lesson Plan

Objective: to increase pupils' understanding of different ways of beginning drama.

Content focus: exploration of individual and social responsibilities towards the old.

Lesson sequence

Introduction – Pupils are introduced to the theme of old age (through photograph, video clip or other stimulus) and asked to reflect on their own beliefs and experiences through whole-group discussion: what responsibility should children have to their elderly parents? should old people automatically live with their children as is the practice in some cultures? is there ever a tension between the interest of the wider family and what is right for the elderly relative? at what point might it be right to put an old person in a home?

Drama focus – The teacher asks the group to imagine that a short scene is being created which will explore this issue. A family who have an elderly relative living with them are divided in their view about whether the relative should continue to live with them or be placed in a home. Two lines of dialogue are distributed which might open the scene. The pupils are asked to discuss possible sub-texts, (intended meanings or what the dialogue might reveal), and the effectiveness of the lines as the opening to a scene.

'I called into the Rookstone Home today – they have a vacancy.'
'Rookstone – but that's miles away.'

'John, would you pack that away? Grandma will be down in a minute.'
'But I'm nearly finished – it will spoil it if I move it now.'

Group tasks

Each group is to plan four different openings to a scene using the techniques listed below – they continue the scene long enough to establish the theme:
- before the dialogue begins, a sequence of actions conveys something which is relevant to the central theme;
- a telephone conversation of which the audience only hears one half – other characters may be in the room;
- direct address to the audience/monologue by one of the characters;
- conversation in which the family are clearing trying to avoid the subject.

Extension work for those who finish early:
- to think of one or more other ways of opening a drama on a similar subject;
- take one of their openings and decide how to continue.

Analysis

The different openings are performed and compared using questions such as: what important information is conveyed? what type of mood is created? how could the mood have been enhanced?

The following lesson plan is based on a familiar theme of family tension between teenager and parent but it is given a different angle because the narrative is not negotiated but presented to the pupils near the beginning of the lesson. Notice, however, the importance of the introductory activity which seeks to engage the pupils with the theme prior to the distribution of the central task.

Lesson Plan

Objectives: to understand the difference between 'narrative' and 'plot' and the importance of dramatic structure in creating meaning.

Content focus: examination of how a breakdown in relationships can affect judgement.

Introduction – Pupils are shown a simple handwritten note from a daughter to her parents making a very strong apology for 'acting in the way she did' and 'being so thoughtless and stupid' but which does not provide details of what she has done. The class are asked to speculate on the reasons for the letter. To each of the suggestions the teacher raises the question, 'what might have prompted her to act in that way'.

Central task

The following simple narrative is distributed:

1. Teenager has a row with her parent about the suitability of her friends.
2. Teenager has another row this time over her clothes.
3. She is invited to go on holiday with her boyfriend.
4. She discusses this invitation with her friends.
5. She decides to go on holiday without asking permission of her parents.
6. Parents assume she is missing and report this fact to the police.
7. Parents and daughter are reunited and reconciled.

In groups the class are asked to create a dramatic plot out of the narrative. In other words they will decide in what different order the story could be told; what elements will be shown or simply reported in dialogue. They are then asked to take one of the scenes and act it out as if it is the opening scene of the drama – do they need to manipulate time as in the use of flashback? Alternatively do they include some of the details and background in the dialogue?

Analysis

The pupils share their ideas and compare the different approaches taken to structuring the drama, examining the strengths of each one. As a follow-up in a subsequent lesson the pupils are introduced to the way playwrights construct dramatic plots.

Integrating elements of drama in lesson planning

It was suggested in this chapter that an exploration of language and meaning can help to reconcile polarities associated with subjectivity and objectivity. Progressive theories which overemphasised subjectivity lead to a narrow range of practices, including in drama. There is no necessary connection on the basis of the discussion in this chapter between quality of experience and a particular approach to drama such as process work. The important issue is the element of negotiation and ownership, whether the focus of the lesson be a particular drama skill or a play text. That does not mean to say that there may not be other arguments, for example based on quality of feeling in favour of one type of practice but that question will need to be deferred to later chapters.

Whereas the work of Slade did privilege experience over structure, the best drama in education practice sought the kind of integration being recommended in this chapter. This, however, was mistakenly seen as a recommendation to *one set of practices* instead of being seen as a *general pedagogic principle*. The final lesson outline which seeks to blend different elements of drama is given here in summary form and is described in more detail in *Meeting the Standards in Secondary English* (Fleming 2001).

Lesson outline

1. The class are divided into pairs and are given a simple role play exercise. Pupil A tries (and eventually succeeds) to persuade pupil B, a close friend, to go somewhere which might not have the approval of his/her parents. The pupils are give a small element of decision making but the activity is tightly structured.

2. A now becomes B's parent who is informing A of an important family gathering which happens to coincide with the previously arranged outing. The pupils are to freeze the action at the point when a row is developing when the parent says something he or she will later regret. The pupils are again invited to fill in details but the content is highly prescribed. Notice, however, that the activity is a little more demanding because the pupils are required to think about the shape and form of the work, the change in tone and the movement towards a climax. The simple constraint of freezing the action acts both as a control measure (to avoid an unproductive slanging match) and to provide more aesthetic shape to the work. The pupils are also asked to think about the relationships involved by creating the final line. This work could be developed by asking pupils to script the exchange.

3. Pupils now combine to create groups of four, ideally mixing boys and girls. An extract from *Romeo and Juliet* is distributed. They are to read it through and work out (a) what it is making the father angry, and (b) what clues there are in the language which tells the father how he should act.

4. The groups are asked to create three tableaux with appropriate positioning and expressions to show exactly where the actors would be standing when the following lines are delivered: 'What still in tears? Evermore show'ring?'; 'I would the fool were married to her grave!'; 'You are to blame, my lord, to rate her so'. This activity gives balanced attention to both content and form. The pupils need to understand what is happening in the scene in order to work out how it might be staged.

5. The pupils are asked to select and underline six or so lines which include all the characters and which convey the essence of the scene. They commit these to memory and bring them to life through action. An example of lines might be as follows:

FATHER: Evermore show'ring?
MOTHER: She will none.
FATHER: I will drag thee there on a hurdle hither.
JULIET: Good father.
FATHER: My fingers itch.
NURSE: You are to blame, my lord.

6. Teacher and pupils discuss the different ways in which the nature of the performance of the scene as a whole can convey different interpretations and meanings. How close is the mother and father to Juliet? What does the line, 'I would the fool were married to her grave' tell us about Juliet's mother? How can the line be delivered differently to convey (a) that this is being said in the heat of the moment, or (b) Juliet's mother is very cold and lacks feeling towards her.

7. The pupils watch a video version of the scene and analyse the way it has been staged, comparing it to their ideas. If they can compare two different versions all the better.

The pupils could be reminded of their own drama work and the way they created a scene which escalated in intensity and change in tone. Does the video performance convey the development to a climax successfully? What was the most impressive aspect of the performance? What was the least helpful? A contrast in styles of dress and setting in two different video versions will also promote useful discussion.

Some of the lessons described in this chapter may appear to be a departure from what is often thought of as traditional drama in education practice. The lessons are not seeking 'high levels of arousal' but are instead seeking at a more modest level to develop understanding of drama and ways in which drama can be structured. A frequent mistake in writing about drama in the past has been to assume that a description of a single lesson is some sort of categorical imperative and representative of how all lessons ought to be taught. This is, in part, a matter of recognising the importance of schemes of work and the relationship between means and ends, the subject of the next chapter.

CHAPTER 3

Planning schemes of work: means and ends

Chapter 1 began with a brief description of two drama lessons both based on the theme of space travel. Each appeared to have a very different emphasis. In one the pupils were asked to work out how to represent through dialogue and movement the landing of a spacecraft on another planet. In the other an imaginary press conference was being held at which the pupils were being questioned about their experiences on another planet. I suspect that some readers may have seen in those two lessons a clear distinction in value and purpose. The first appears superficial and aimless, empty of any significant content. In contrast, the second lesson seems to have far more potential to challenge pupils' thinking. The intention, however, was not to draw crude parallels of that kind. To make an informed judgement about these lessons it is necessary to have more information about how they fit into a syllabus or scheme of work, particularly with regard to broad educational aims.

The discussion which follows will be relevant both to the planning of syllabuses (or programmes of study) and schemes of work. The difference between 'schemes' and 'syllabuses' is primarily a matter of degree but there are some important distinctions which need to be identified. A scheme of work might consist of a module lasting for a limited number of weeks. The term 'syllabus' or 'programme of study' is used here to refer to a specification of work which will last for a key stage or for the whole of compulsory schooling. It is the overall drama programme which will provide breadth and balance for pupils, not an individual short scheme of work which might be fairly narrow in scope. It is useful to keep this distinction in mind because it is easy to assume that one scheme or even one single lesson is representative of a teacher's entire method of working.

Schemes of work

It is only fairly recently that writers on drama have turned their attention to the importance of medium and long-term planning in drama. In the 1970s and 1980s attention focused far more on teaching of individual lessons or short sequences of lessons with much less concentration on how these should fit into a broader scheme. There are historical, practical and theoretical reasons for this. Many of the leading exponents of drama in education were lecturing in higher education or working as local authority advisers rather than teaching in schools. Most lessons were taught as one-off projects and the question of how these might fit into a scheme of work was rarely considered. It was thought to be innovative and impressive enough that the pioneers of drama were teaching children at all; colleagues in other subjects were content to theorise and offer advice without engaging in practice or basing recommendations on systematic research.

Schemes of work were also considered less important because there was some uncertainty about the proper place of drama in the curriculum. Arguments about whether drama should be conceived as a subject or method inevitably distracted attention from what drama as a subject with a definite syllabus should look like. Similarly it could be argued that the theatre/drama debate distracted attention from consideration of schemes of work; specification of the content of a drama syllabus would have felt like a reduction in the importance of process and too much of a concession to advocates of theatre practice. Even examination syllabuses did not need precise specification of content because the requirements were often phrased in very general terms.

Another reason for the emphasis on individual lessons rather than schemes of work is that much less consideration was given to questions related to progression and continuity prior to the introduction of the National Curriculum in the United Kingdom. Since 1989 many writers on drama have been concerned with more long-term planning, even though drama did not secure separate subject status in the National Curriculum. In contrast, publications in the 1970s and 1980s gave examples of individual lessons or provided discussion of the aims of drama but paid much less attention to the question of what a sustained syllabus should look like over a period of weeks or years.

Neelands (1998:6) has pointed out that the absence of a legislative framework for drama in England and Wales is both a strength and a weakness:

> The strength is that, in the absence of a national agreement about a drama curriculum, schools are free to design a curriculum for drama that is particularly responsive to local needs: to the local context for drama provided by a particular school representing a particular community.

Harland *et al.* (2000) found in their research a mixed reaction to the National Curriculum among teachers of arts subjects. A number reported that the requirements 'had helped them to clarify the content of the curriculum, and introduce new processes and activities – thereby extending the effectiveness of the arts education they provided' (p.340). Others found it restrictive and commented on the lack of freedom and choice available to both teachers and pupils.

> To write a full-scale scheme of work and to actually put all the aims and objectives, to write down the homeworks and to actually know exactly how many homeworks have got to be done in the term etc., takes a long time. While you are doing that, you are not thinking, you are not sparking and coming up with brand new ideas. (p.341)

Some teachers felt the National Curriculum brought more structure and purpose to their work.

> A lot of staff had an awful lot of trouble with the National Curriculum when it came in because a lot of the arts staff worked intuitively. I think it would be fair to say that many of the arts staff would walk down the corridor on the way to their lesson and say 'What shall we do?', and be thinking what they were going to do on their way down to the lesson. Now we have specific modules of work which are designed to last between six and eight weeks... (p.340)

If drama had secured separate subject status in 1989 no doubt there would have been considerable controversy about defining attainment targets and programmes of study but there would at least have been a focus for national discussion. It is clear that the introduction of a National Curriculum for drama would not have been welcomed by all drama teachers as many enjoy the freedom of working outside these structures. As one of those interviewed puts it:

> the brilliant thing about not being on the National Curriculum – you can do what you need to do. You can tailor-make things for classes, you can go off on a tangent, and you can do cross-curricular with art if you decided – you have that flexibility with it. (p.342)

The appreciation of the need for a flexible approach to planning embodied in this quotation has been characteristic of much drama writing. Its most extreme manifestation was adopted by teachers who began each individual lesson with the question 'what do you want to do a play about?'. This does indeed seem a radical methodology in the current educational climate but some might argue that this sort of approach embodies the true spirit of Doll's postmodern paradigm described in Chapter 2. It does seek to promote the engagement and true ownership of the drama by the participants.

This focus on individual lessons in the 1970s and early 1980s had significant consequences. It meant that much tortured discussion took place over the purpose of drama conceived in terms of one or two lessons. This proved to be a significant Achilles' heel of drama in education because it proved very difficult to identify with any degree of certainty the value of a small number of lessons in terms of learning outcomes related to content. How do we articulate the learning objectives of a drama project based on a theme such as 'Murder at the Disco'? Not surely to teach pupils how to commit a murder at a disco, nor to ensure that in future visits to discos they will take precautions against getting murdered themselves. General objectives such as the development of personal qualities like 'confidence' associated with personal and social education seemed to hark back to the drama of the 1950s and 1960s and were not considered suitable outcomes of 'drama for learning'. To conceive lessons in terms of drama 'skills' (voice projection, movement, mime) seemed highly reductive.

Another consequence of focusing on individual lessons rather than schemes of work was the implicit assumption that the type of learning objectives which related to a particular lesson were characteristic of all others. The focus on individual lessons did not give sufficient recognition to the fact that in a drama scheme of work different *types* of lesson might be taught: that a particular skill might well be the object of some lessons without a teacher necessarily subscribing to a reductive concept of the subject. It is quite reasonable to have different types of lessons all subscribing to the same ends, a concept which needs some detailed discussion.

Ends

Why use the word 'ends' rather than 'aims'? There is an obvious stylistic reason in that the balance between 'means' and 'ends' has a familiar ring. There is another more substantial reason however. The term 'ends' suggests a more fundamental concern with questions of value and deep purpose. Aims and objectives abound in educational discourse: schemes of work and lesson plans will not pass the external scrutiny of mentors, head teachers, tutors or OFSTED inspectors unless they contain an obligatory statement of educational purpose. But these are often limited in their scope and, if thought about seriously, invite further questions. An aim such as 'to enable pupils to become "dramatically literate"' or 'enable pupils to understand aspects of drama and theatre' begs the question 'to what purpose?' To make money? To advance political propaganda? To prepare for a career in the theatre? Questions of value can easily be overlooked in a statement of aims.

This is not surprising. We live in an age in which complex questions about educational aims have been reduced to a matter of 'raising standards' as if, according to Blake *et al.* (2000:xi) 'educational achievement were no different from that of a football team pulling clear of the relegation zone or becoming a contender for promotion'. League tables comparing schools and local authorities, target setting and inspections give the illusion that every participant in the system has a clear sense of common purpose. However, everything seems to be defined not by any real grasp of value but simply by what is its opposite.

The university department may be exemplary (by the standards of quality assurance), the school may be a beacon (having come out of its inspection better than most): but a beacon or example of quite *what* it is generally hard to say. There is a sense here that what is valuable is defined by contradistinction to its opposite (the merely satisfactory, or even the failing).   (p.xii)

The authors see in this formulation of value as *the opposite of its opposite* what Nietzsche saw as the core of nihilism. In *The Will to Power*, Nietzsche writes that 'The highest values have devalued themselves. There is no goal. There is no answer to the question 'why?''.

> He believes this is the state of affairs of his time. Values have become merely conventional: they are experienced as external to us, as things we do not recognise ourselves in or identify ourselves with. Political programmes proceed under their own momentum. It is the smooth running of the system which thus becomes by default, the chief goal and end.   (Blake *et al.* 2000:xi)

Blake *et al.* write of the nihilism which characterises education in much of the English-speaking world and particularly in the UK at the present time. In their earlier book *Thinking Again: Education After Postmodernism* they draw on Lyotard's concept of 'performativity', the obsession with 'efficiency' and 'effectiveness', which has 'parted company' from questions of 'what we should be trying to achieve'.

> Under performativity, deliberation over ends is eclipsed…All kinds of business and activity are measured and ranked against each other, with ever less concern for the rationale for doing so.   (p.1)

One of the accolades that inspectors sometimes bestow on a school in England is that it represents 'good value for money', although it is not always clear what 'good value' means.

In drama the absorption in technique and skill or undue emphasis on form and structure can easily deflect attention from consideration of questions of value and purpose. The important point here is not to resolve the question of ends by a simple statement of aims embodied in a cliché or some sort of 'mission statement' nor to seek an explanation by defining an alternative 'grand narrative' but to examine different approaches to the subject in some detail. One of the underlying themes of this book relates to questions of language and meaning. Reliance on a simple mission statement or aim betrays a naive faith in the transparency of language; as if a group (whether it be a company, school or department) because they are 'united' around a single slogan will necessarily share the same intentions and beliefs. This is to expect too much of language. Most mission statements are bland and incontrovertible. It is only through shared exploration of beliefs and interpretation of practice, or participation in an educational 'form of life' that real communication and shared understanding can take place can take place (Wittgenstein 1953:19).

Approaches to drama

A bald statement of the aims of drama often fails to convey the underlying assumptions or texture of beliefs from which it derives or which it implies. The discussion of approaches to drama here will draw on Cox's models for the teaching of English. The publication of the National Curriculum for English was based on the report of the Cox Committee (Cox 1989) in which five models of English were identified. Since their publication, these have been repeatedly quoted in publications about the subject to the extent that it is difficult to read any extensive discussion of English teaching without coming across some reference to Cox's models. They have been frequently criticised but they have also provided a useful focus for discussion as well as research (Goodwyn 1992, Hardman and Williamson 1993). They will used here to explore broadly different ways of thinking about drama:

- cultural heritage
- personal growth
- cross curricular
- adult needs
- cultural analysis.

Drama as cultural heritage

A 'cultural heritage' model emphasises the responsibility of schools to 'lead children to an appreciation of those works of literature that have been widely regarded as amongst the finest in the language' (Cox 1991:22). Applied to drama this would inevitably mean focusing on the work of key playwrights of the last 500 years. One of the arguments for making scripted plays and particularly 'classics' the main focus of the drama curriculum is articulated in the following quotation:

> The stylistic perfection of love expressed through the sonnet Romeo and Juliet share on the first meeting, or the fumbling silences as Lopakhin takes his leave of Varya in *The Cherry Orchard*, are just random examples of the kind of density of human experience collected within our dramatic history whose range and depth of meaning leave even the most accomplished role-playing far behind.
>
> (Hornbrook 1989:108)

What is not recognised here is that access to the 'density of human experience' within great plays will depend on how they are taught. There is a false polarisation here between 'role-playing' and 'working with text' which does not attend sufficiently to the importance of means (to be discussed later in this chapter). There is an implicit assumption that exposure to the classics will automatically provide access to a density of human experience which any experienced teacher will know is far from being the case. Clark and Goode (1999:11) have criticised what they describe as Hornbrook's 'high art' model revealed in this same quotation:

> We do not seek to rubbish the canon of 'high art' but instead argue the need to challenge the cultural hierarchy which places more importance on the products of art processes than on valuing those processes themselves.

The distinction between process and product will be discussed in more detail in Chapter 7 but it is worth recognising here that the access to the density of human experience in classics texts may be through integrating different forms of role play and process work. An approach of that kind is more likely to prevent the type of alienation which a naive approach to drama as cultural heritage entails. Lyas (1997) writes very convincingly of the 'sense of deprivation' many people feel in relation to the arts, people who feel they have 'missed out'. He makes the important point that it is not so much that they are deprived of an aesthetic life but they are deprived of access to art. Most people's lives are full of aesthetic choices and experiences found in everyday activities such as choosing clothes, dancing, listening to music and walking in the countryside. However, there is a barrier to those items which are held up as aesthetic icons.

> they worry because what they do get from art is often derided, as when their genuine delight in the scenes painted by Constable is written off as irrelevant compared with something mysteriously characterised as 'the formal features' of a painting. Someone, too, deeply moved by Auden's beautiful *Lullaby*, is told instead to attend to some hocus-pocus involving such barbarisms as 'signifier' and 'metonymy'.   (ibid: 4).

Lyas refers to the 'bedrock' of 'spontaneous reactions' which we make from early infancy which provide the foundation for a life enriched by art. Marching up and down, listening to stories, attempting to paint a picture, watching the clouds are as natural as eating and sleeping and are the 'beginning of what would issue, were education systems designed to reinforce rather than to frustrate our aesthetic development...' (ibid:1). It is important to recognise that 'high art' has its origins in natural activity.

It is not unreasonable to suggest that one of the aims of a drama curriculum should be to intitiate pupils into a cultural (and intercultural) heritage of great plays and the history of the theatre. This is partly a question of ends. If one purpose of teaching drama is 'to inspire a life-long love of theatre as a way of enriching pupils' lives and coming to terms with their own experiences' this has more significant implications than a less fundamental aim such as 'to introduce pupils to the classics'. But it also has implications for means. The 'bedrock activity' which forms the basis for appreciating the 'density of human experience' to be found in dramatic literature lies in pupils' own natural dramatic playing.

Drama as personal growth

A 'personal growth' view of English tends to emphasise the pupil as a creative and imaginative individual developing primarily through an engagement with literature and personal creative writing. If applied broadly to drama teaching this category subsumes two distinctive traditions in drama teaching. The approach to drama which emerged in the 1950s and 1960s largely through the work of Slade and Way reflected wider educational thinking at the time. Spontaneous, creative, self expression was valued as a balance to the mechanical acquisition of knowledge which had preoccupied earlier generations. Drama as personal growth was realised in the natural dramatic play of children and its value was closely associated with the acquisition of personal qualities. Because personal growth tended to be associated with natural self expression, the role of the teacher was minimised. The term 'personal growth' therefore often carries an implicit assumption about means because it tends to refer to a methodology of teaching as much as it does to a statement of the purpose of drama teaching.

Histories of drama teaching almost always distinguish a 'personal growth' model from 'drama for learning' or 'drama for understanding', the approach which developed in the 1970s and 1980s. However, 'drama for learning/understanding' can be subsumed under the broad category of 'personal growth' if the term is used more as an expression of educational purpose, of ends rather than means. If drama is used to increase the understanding of the participants then this in some sense is contributing to their personal growth. Here the purpose is not primarily the development of personal qualities but the development of understanding through coming to terms with life experiences. Histories of drama which mark the move from 'personal growth' to 'drama for learning' are highlighting a contrast in means, largely focusing on a difference in the role of the teacher. The distinction is important because the 'language games' involved can be a source of confusion (see Chapter 8).

Drama as a cross-curricular subject

One of the issues which has dogged the history of drama teaching is the so-called 'drama as subject or method' debate. The question was not so much a matter of choosing between these alternatives but to question whether focus on drama as a means of teaching other subjects was in some ways a cause of the erosion of separate subject identity. The reasonable view seems to be that there is no reason why drama should not exist as a separate subject and be employed as a methodology to teach other subjects. After all, literacy, numeracy and other key skills are frequently thought of in cross-curricular terms. The problem, however, with the cross-curricular view is that it can erode the status of drama as a *specialism* which is rather different from drama's identity as a *subject*. Its subject status is a matter of whether or not it has a separate place in the curriculum. Its status as a specialism recognises the need for teachers and pupils to have particular kinds of expertise in drama.

This is not a straightforward matter. It was suggested in Chapter 1 that one of the assumptions underlying early drama in education practice which is still implicit in much process drama work was that a teacher with any group could produce high quality work irrespective of their level of experience and skill. Because drama has its origins in dramatic playing there is an assumption that drama is a natural activity which does not have to be taught. This view underpinned Slade's approach which made a virtue out of the lack of intervention of the teacher but it was also implicit in drama in education practice because the concept of 'teaching' was given meaning by reference to the learning or understanding which came about as a result of engagement in the drama. It has always been one of the positive strengths of drama as a school subject, as conceived by drama in education practitioners, that it is accessible to everyone and not the preserve of a chosen or talented elite.

However, this view of drama has negative consequences as well. It often meant that drama when used in cross-curricular contexts resulted in pupils producing endless improvised skits in small groups as a break from the more serious business of the syllabus. There is a need for drama specialists whether at primary or secondary level to be cautious about the casual use of drama to teach a variety of subjects. It would be more appropriate to use teamwork and collaboration between teachers in order to implement cross-curricular drama. An effective drama policy in a school would provide a focus and structure for this to happen.

Drama as meeting adult needs

Because drama in education derives from a liberal humanist or progressive curriculum tradition, there has been very little discussion of the direct vocational relevance of drama as a subject. According to Hornbrook,

> for years drama-in-education at secondary level shrunk from the spectre of vocational training. To the student who might actually want to work in the theatre, the developmental vocabulary of 'the drama process' has little or nothing to say. Realistically of course, few students achieve the status of professional actors. However, more might wish to pursue an interest awakened at school in an amateur capacity; for others, involvement in school drama may lead them into films or television, or into jobs as property makers, scene painters or theatre adminstrators.
>
> (Hornbrook 1991:6)

It is not necessary to react too strongly to this kind of view, either in a positive or negative way. It would be reductive in the extreme to see the purpose or end of drama education to reside in vocational objectives. But neither is it unreasonable to take some notice of such considerations when determining the place of drama within the school curriculum. What is of more significance is that the relevance of drama to employers goes beyond the direct employment of pupils in arts-related jobs. In the Secondary Heads Association survey (1998:36) almost half of the 688 respondents from schools did not see drama as a vocational subject but considered the most valuable educational element to be the 'spin-off' as shown by personal development, confidence, team-building, taking responsibility, self-esteem, which were all seen as important for any career.

The concept of 'adult needs' can be extended beyond the notion of vocational relevance to the importance of preparing pupils for a rich cultural life. The wider concept of adult needs draws attention to pupils as a potential theatre audience. The importance of 'responding' to drama will be discussed in more detail Chapter 5.

Drama as cultural analysis

In Cox's models of English the cultural analysis view emphasises the role of English in helping children towards a 'critical understanding of the world and cultural environment in which they live'. Children should know about the 'processes by which meanings are conveyed, and about the ways in which print and other media carry values' (Cox 1991:22). Applied to drama, the phrase 'critical understanding of the world' would not be out of place in a personal growth model but the change of emphasis is more on understanding how meanings are constructed and conveyed than on personal growth through expression.

A similar contrast is found in English teaching between traditional approaches to reading and a more recent emphasis in media education. Hardman (2001:154) has pointed out that whereas reading literature is seen as 'a process of developing pupils' receptiveness and responsiveness to something which is regarded as being morally educative', reading the media is about 'encouraging pupils to resist or see through the deception in the texts'.

> In studying and creating media texts, pupils are asked to consider the ways in which audiences are targeted and addressed. Therefore much more emphasis is placed on social accounts of the ways in which social texts are produced and read in contrast to English's traditional concerns with the individual reader's personal response.   (ibid:156)

Hardman goes on to point out that the different conceptions of the two subjects has lead to differences in pedogogical practice reflected in the terminology of English and Media Studies syllabuses. Differences in their notions of 'reading' and 'writing' become apparent.

In English, in their reading, pupils are required to 'understand' and 'evaluate', to 'respond imaginatively', to 'enjoy' and 'appreciate' what they read. In writing, they are expected to 'communicate effectively', to 'articulate experience and express what is felt and imagined'. In Media Studies syllabuses, the emphasis is very much on developing 'critical analysis' of the ways in which media texts are 'constructed' so that pupils become competent consumers of the media by learning to read visual images, codes, conventions and grammar. The concept of the constructed nature of media products in which everything is a mediated view is therefore fundamental to media education.   (ibid:156)

The distinction drawn here can be usefully applied to drama. A comparison between cultural heritage and personal growth models can lead to an oversimplified polarisation which at its crudest centres on whether or not play texts should be part of the drama curriculum. However, there is no reason why inclusion of plays should exclude aims related to personal growth, particularly in the light of literary theory which emphases the role of the reader in the creation of meaning. But there is a difference in emphasis between engaging in drama for the purpose of learning and understanding about human situations (traditional drama in education aims) and engaging in drama to learn about how meanings are constructed. It is a difference in emphasis rather than kind because the construction of meaning is always related to a specific human context. These differences transcend the issue of whether or not texts should be used in the classroom. Contemporary practice in drama teaching is likely to have more focus on construction and deconstruction of meaning by the pupils than in traditional drama in education practice.

Means

We live in an educational age in which aims and objectives are highly valued. No scheme of work or lesson plan will pass scrutiny by external agencies unless aims and objectives are clearly specified. In England one of the criteria for a good lesson specified by OFSTED (the government inspection agency) is that its objectives are expressed clearly. It was also suggested that despite this apparent focus on educational purpose, questions of value can easily be ignored. It is one thing to clarify what pupils should know, understand and be able to do; it is another matter to ask why. It is also possible to overestimate the importance of specifying narrow outcomes, and undervalue the impact of teaching methodology.

Some approaches to rational planning of the curriculum contain an implicit view that the relationship between means and ends is always contingent. The curriculum planner or teacher must identify a particular aim or set of objectives and then choose the method which suits their experience, preferences or style. The cliché that something is only a 'means to and end' is entirely misleading if it implies that choice of means is of little real significance. The relationship between means and ends is more complex.

Hornbrook (1998:63) published a summary of a scheme of work for 11 to 14 year olds which placed more emphasis on knowledge than many previous schemes for drama. The focus was as follows: Year 7 pupils (ages 11 to 12): Indian theatre, medieval theatre, mask drama, comedy, Elizabethan theatre, street theatre; Year 8 pupils (ages 12 to 13): naturalism and realism, tv drama, melodrama, absurdism, comedy and Brecht; Year 9 pupils (ages 13 to 14): tragedy, Indian drama, contemporary plays, Elizabethan theatre, tv drama, theatre in education.

The emphasis on knowledge seemed to be an even greater challenge to the tradition of drama in education than his previous writing. To many drama teachers this scheme seemed the ultimate betrayal of the tradition of drama in education. But a different reaction is possible. Beyond the statement of the proposed syllabus in the book there is little indication of what form the teaching will take apart from a suggestion that in the context of the melodrama work, the teacher 'might explain how candlelight was replaced by gas in the nineteenth century, and what effect this had on the performance style of the time . . .' (ibid: 64).

Without any indication of 'means' there is little clue as to how the drama experience will be realised in the classroom. It is precisely the insights derived from drama in education practice which would translate the proposed syllabus into meaningful learning. It is only necessary to imagine the kind of teaching and educational outcomes Heathcote or Bolton would develop given the brief to translate the content into a set of coherent educational experiences for young people. Would not, for example, 'mask drama' lend itself to an approach based on mantle of the expert? Might not a theme such as 'time travel ' (using elements of process drama) be a valuable way in to medieval theatre? The separation of means from ends will always diminish the educational experience because 'means' are a significant determining factor on what the ends turn out to be in practice.

Attempts to categorise 'means' run the risk of isolating one method of working from another. If a 'script based' approach is contrasted with a 'conventions' approach, the implication may be that work on script will not use such techniques as tableau, questioning in role, teacher in role, etc. Similarly if 'living through' drama is conceived as something entirely distinct from small group play making, this view does not recognise that the quality of pupils' own devising will inevitably be enhanced by an experience of whole-group, spontaneous improvisation.

Hornbrook (1998:65) concludes one of his chapters in *On The Subject of Drama* with the following observation about a primary school production of *A Midsummer Night's Dream*.

A whole class of ten year olds had been involved in rehearsing, learning lines, making costumes and scenery and now performed the play to parents and friends. It was a memorable occasion, and as I sat there I cast my mind ahead to when in the September following, those children would have arrived in their secondary schools, probably to drama as a timetabled subject. What sort of experience would face them then, I speculated? Would the girls who played Titania with such verve and the boy who had laboured over painted trees and cardboard crowns in between learning his lines as Demetrius have their emerging command of the craft of drama recognised, sustained and built on? Or would the confidence and prowess so powerfully evident in that primary school playground be allowed to lie fallow in the interest of an undifferentiated programme of role-play and improvisation?

There is no reason to doubt the sincerity of this account but without any description of 'means' it is difficult to make any judgement of this work as an educational experience. Without any description of 'ends' other than 'mount a production of a Shakespeare play' it is difficult to establish educational purpose. The fact that it is a Shakespeare play with primary school children provides a form of tacit authority which seems to suggest there is no need for further explanation. Replace the title *A Midsummer Night's Dream* with 'A Play About a Teddy Bear' and the paragraph does not have quite the same ring. In both cases, however, understanding of significant content will depend on process, on teaching method. Even if a fairly traditional approach to play production is adopted, the rehearsal techniques must involve some sort of workshop activities if the pupils are to be engaged with the work.

Planning schemes of work

The approaches outlined in the previous sections have implications for broad approaches to the planning of drama. Planning schemes of work can be undertaken in terms of theme, project, script, genres and styles and skills (see Table 3.1 opposite). A thematic approach has tended to be more closely associated with personal growth models of drama where the emphasis is very much on the content of the drama (bullying, school, family conflicts). One advantage of this approach to planning is that it gives unity and meaning to the pupils' experiences. However, it may obscure any real sense of progression for them or reduce attention to the acquisition of specific skills. It also tends to emphasise 'making' and tends to place less emphasis on responding to drama.

Another advantage of a thematic approach is that pupils can be given choice over content. Owens and Barber (1997:13) rightly point out the benefits of providing choice in this way:

> The group members have a real sense of ownership of the content, it means something to them and so they are likely to be motivated. It keeps the teacher working on new ideas and is in this sense a creative and educational challenge.

Table 3.1

Planning approach	Advantage	Disadvantage	Theoretical underpinning
Thematic (e.g. the environment, pirates, space travel)	Pupil centred. Places emphasis on meaning.	May be difficult for pupils to see progression. Emphasis on responding to drama may be marginalised.	Personal growth. Experiential theories.
Project (e.g. theatre in education, researching and devising a play for performance, work based on other subjects)	Allows flexibility. Usually has a clear goal.	Focus on outcome may detract from process.	Cultural analysis.
Text based (either play texts or scripts written by pupils)	Provides a clear focus. Ensures that the drama content is accessible to public scrutiny.	May duplicate work on the English curriculum.	Cultural heritage. Reader response.
Genres and styles (e.g. melodrama, masks)	Brings more breadth to the drama syllabus.	Unless approached in the right way, may be difficult for pupils to engage.	Cultural analysis.
Skills	Objectives are clear. Planning for assessment is more straightforward.	Runs the risk of marginalising any significant content. May be reductive.	Adult needs.

A purely text based approach provides both a clear focus for the drama and a more tangible indication of what the work is about for external scrutiny but may sacrifice pupil engagement (depending of course on the specific approach in the classroom). It also is less appropriate for young pupils or for those for whom reading is difficult. The relationship of drama to English in the curriculum also needs to be considered. This factor has been underestimated in many discussions about the place of drama in the curriculum and its status as a separate subject. Drama has always had its place in the English curriculum as a literary rather than dramatic discipline where plays were studied in terms of their themes and characters rather than extending consideration to how meaning is actually created in performance. Increasingly, however, English examination syllabuses are urging that plays should be approached as drama rather than purely as literary texts.

The term 'project' is being used here as an umbrella term to refer to specific work which extends over a period of time but is not specifically related to a theme. This category inevitably overlaps with the others. For example, a theatre in education project or the devising of a pantomime for performance could just as easily be classed as an example of a genre or style approach. The separate category however is a reminder that valuable drama can be developed in cross-curricular contexts and also embraces the type of work that can be built around a visit to a theatre performance. It can also be used to refer to the devising of a scripted performance from improvisation or building a semi-fictional play through research.

An approach based on genres or dramatic forms might include topics such as theatre in education, physical theatre or theatre of the absurd. As with several of the approaches listed here it is more likely to be of value with older pupils. Again the categories overlap because 'physical theatre' is not necessarily distinct from a text based approach. According to Irwin (2000:27) the introduction of physical theatre leads to 'alternative and accessible methods of performance, improvisation, script-writing, devising and design'.

A skills focus speaks for itself although it is worth emphasising the point made in Chapter 1 that often objectives specified as drama skills provide a weak focus for the outcome of drama. Isolating skills from context is not easy and many of the drama conventions which are identified as a form of skill in the literature are readily acquired by pupils of all ages given the right motivation. The category however does raise questions over whether the teaching of specific skills should arise in context or be the subject of a systematic programme.

These approaches are not intended to be set up as discrete or competing categories. They are presented here as reminders of possibilities rather than as recommendations for particular types of practice. Despite surface appearances, they should be seen as *organisational strategies* rather than representative of different ideologies of drama. In practice the different approaches will enrich each other. One of the values of paying attention to 'ends' is that it becomes apparent that all of these approaches can be subsumed under the broad heading of 'personal growth'. That is of course as long as that term is being used as a statement of educational purpose, e.g. 'coming to terms with experience' rather than implying a particular movement in educational history associated with natural development and non-intervention by the teacher. All of these approaches are likely to contribute to the pupils' personal growth depending on how they are taught. Ultimately the educational experience for the pupils will depend on means as much as on ends.

It is for that reason that planning a scheme of work needs to be seen (either metaphorically or literally) in terms of a 'matrix' rather than a linear sequence which forces us to think simply in terms of successive themes or texts. A simple theme such as 'families' may provide all sorts of opportunities to work on text extracts (e.g. *Romeo and Juliet*), to translate play texts into performance, to help pupils respond to drama, to acquire specific skills in devising drama (e.g. work on exposition), as well as using different drama conventions. Similarly a scheme of work structured around a specific text (*Romeo and Juliet*) may well make use of such conventions as teacher in role, devising and spontaneous improvisation.

As Winston and Tandy (2001:116) have pointed out, when planning a sequence of lessons for young pupils (Year 2 of the primary school) drama is likely to be integrated into other curriculum areas 'with limited discrete objectives'. As pupils get older the objectives and assessment criteria will become more drama specific. The discussion of schemes of work inevitably raises issues to do with progression and assessment which will be discussed in subsequent chapters.

It is worth pointing out here however that as well as keeping a broad framework of progression in mind in terms of pupils' learning and understanding in the subject, the concept of progression has relevance to 'pedagogic design'. A scheme of work is more than just a collection of ideas for lessons but needs to be thought through in terms of pupils' engagement, response and growing independence (that is, each individual scheme is virtually a microcosm for pupils' 'macro' development in the subject). A scheme of work, just as much as an individual lesson, needs to balance structure and experience. In other words a scheme of work on a play text might begin with a more accessible experience of 'living through' improvisation with teacher in role in order to introduce the particular theme. When planning a scheme of work the first lessons are vital to capture the pupils' interest and involvement. After that the work may well develop its own momentum and take some of the pressure away from the teacher to expend enormous amounts of energy every single lesson. The traditional model of drama in education practice was exhausting for the teacher who retained responsibility for devising, creating and structuring the drama and ensuring the appropriate 'depth of feeling'. This can be described as a search for the right quality of 'internal experience' as opposed to being satisfied with routine behaviour associated with the creation of outer forms. The distinction between internal and external experiences requires closer attention.

CHAPTER 4

Assessing drama: internal and external experiences

It is nearing the climax of the lesson. The guards slowly approach the prisoners' cell. They stop outside and discover that one of them has lost his keys. The senior officer barks out a command, 'Fool, check the cell'. The guards go inside. They body-search the prisoners and check under the blankets without finding anything. When they leave the prisoners gather round and in whispers make their final plans for escape. They notice the look on the face of one of their fellow prisoners and start to get suspicious. Suddenly the voice of one of the guards is heard, 'Where are the keys?' The stool pigeon stands up very slowly and indicates one of the prisoners. 'He's got them sir.' The retort comes back slowly and with great bitterness, 'Swine, you swine'. The stool pigeon crouches down with his head in his hands.

This scene comes from the BBC film made in 1971 *Three Looms Waiting* based on the work of Dorothy Heathcote. For this project she was teaching a group of teenaged boys in an 'approved' school for young offenders. The film and this particular lesson had an enormous impact on the teaching of drama and much has been written about it since (Davis 1985, Morgan and Saxton 1987, Fleming 1994:16, Bolton 1998:221). Concepts such as 'engagement', 'depth', 'moment of awe' were often applied to the moment described here. We will return to this lesson in Chapter 7 in order to analyse it from a contemporary perspective, examining the way meaning is constructed rather than just marvelling at the depth of feeling of the participants. It will be used in the discussion in this chapter, however, to raise issues related to the assessment of drama.

One of the reasons this lesson became so influential was the level of involvement shown by the pupils involved. For many drama in education practitioners it represented the ideal to which all drama teaching aspired. The level of absorption and ownership of the participants, and the quality of the experience was without doubt very impressive. Let us imagine a hypothetical case in which a different group of pupils are 'coached' into re-enacting exactly the same sequence as happens in the climax to this lesson. When I have mentioned this possibility in lectures it has been pointed out to me that this simply would not be feasible; the circumstances here are unique and it would be impossible to replicate them exactly. That may well be the case but it is a logical rather than a realistic hypothesis. It is possible to *imagine* that a group of pupils are given exactly the same lines and mindlessly drilled to perform the same actions as the young boys in this sequence, even if the likelihood of being able to do this is very remote.

The key question in relation to this hypothetical case is how do we distinguish the 'real' from the 'replicated' experience given that the external action is identical in both? One of the major contributions made by early exponents of drama in education was to highlight the importance of the quality of the experience of the participants in the drama. Previous approaches to the subject took a variety of forms: the repetition of physical actions ('get up...yawn...wash behind your ears'), acting out of scripted lines under the direction of the teacher ('say those words a little more angrily and toss your head slightly as you say them'), small group dramatic playing ('in your group act out your journey to school') and various other manifestations. What many of them had in common was an emphasis on getting the external actions to look right without any real attention to the quality of feeling of the participants. With the advent of drama in education practice, the 'feeling engagement' and understanding of the pupils became key components in the evaluation of the drama. However, if the internal experiences are important how do we take these into account when making judgements about the drama? This is a question which clearly has implications for assessment.

Internal and external

The distinction between internal and external experiences is still an important one to writers on drama:

> It is perhaps not surprising that some educators have tried to fit the dynamic and evolving drama curriculum into an outcome-oriented programme, with the outcomes essentially being those skills and attitudes which can be observed and measured, rather the intrinsic changes which happen inside humans when they experience a work of art.
> (Taylor 2000:74).

According to Clark and Goode (1999:13) the drama process is 'a mediation between our inner selves and the real world'. Nicholson (2000:15) points out that 'students are not assessed on their private values, beliefs or attitudes, but on their actual and visible contributions to the development and realization of the drama'. The development of 'drama in education' can in part be described as a move away from an earlier emphasis on external, public and to some writers 'superficial' elements to a focus on genuine depth and feeling. This focus on the 'internal' has been one of the criticisms launched by Hornbrook at the tradition of drama in education seen by him as a continuation of a romantic tradition. One of the past legacies from which he wants to break free is what he sees as an excessive emphasis on 'private' or 'internal' experiences. 'By emphasising spontaneity over the acquisition of knowledge and skills' the arts are turned into 'psychological processes' (Hornbrook 1998:10). Romanticism 'internalised art, shifting the emphasis away from the skilled exercise of a craft, from production' (p.58). Post-war thinking about art education 'turned us away from thinking of art as a matter of making and appraising socially valued products and towards the idea of art as a therapeutic engagement with the inner world of individuals' (Hornbrook 1989:69). The 'private, dispositional outcomes of educational drama' are contrasted with 'the demonstrably public ones of the theatre' (p.71).

Many of the polar concepts which are the subject of this book underlie these criticisms: process and product, feeling and form, structure and experience, public and private. At the core of these distinctions however is that between 'internal' and 'external' experiences which is one of the more philosophically challenging dualities. However, before examining the theoretical implications underlying these concepts it is worth considering the issues from a rather more straightforward point of view. If a concept of aesthetic education is to make any sense, it is imperative that as teachers we attend to the nature of the experience which the pupils are having. Not to do so will be accepting that a valid drama experience will be had by pupils who are merely mouthing lines without any understanding and engagement, or mindlessly painting scenery without any sense of meaning and purpose. To accept this view is to return to the practices which drama teachers have sought to escape from for 50 years.

On the other hand Hornbrook's questioning of the emphasis on the 'internal' also seems to make sense. If we give credence and value to what is essentially hidden and private this makes any attempt at justification or evaluation invalid. Hence the significance of locating this discussion in a chapter about assessment. Assessment after all is about public accountability, it is about making judgements and justifying them in a public arena. From a theoretical point of view we seem to be torn between subscribing to a form of behaviourism (whereby only external actions are considered important) or being subject to accusations of some sort of romantic mysticism or, even worse, philosophical dualism.

The concept of dualism introduces another set of polarities: mentalism and behaviourism, body and mind, subjectivity and objectivity (Sluga and Stern 1996:336). It is not difficult to find writers who simply assert that such forms of dualism have been transcended and now have no relevance. But as Cooper (1990:80) has written, 'the rejection of (this) dualism has become something of a cliché among writers who are described as "post modern" in outlook' and that 'nowhere is it made clear what is being dismissed or deconstructed'. It is for that reason it is important to locate the present discussion in the context of practical issues related to assessment rather than conduct an abstract debate. The concept of dualism is of little relevance unless its full implications are explored. As with so many of the questions raised in this book, the writing of Wittgenstein is illuminating because his thinking, for all it may appear somewhat abstract, is grounded in real life and action.

Wittgenstein's writing was largely responsible for the revolution in philosophy which dispensed with what has been termed the 'inner facade' of Western thought (Finch 1995:74).

> The sweep and scope of Wittgenstein's innovation in destroying what he called the 'house of cards' of the 'inner world' becomes evident when we realise that every single Western philosopher since Plato has accepted in some form or another the conception of *mental contents of the mind or consciousness* (as has every modern psychologist). All have assumed the existence of images, ideas, thoughts, impressions, notions, concepts or the like.   (p.77)

The mistake was to assume that words like 'understanding', 'thinking', 'imagining' must be describing some inner mental state to which the human subject has access. In order to grasp this point we need to bracket out our common sense view that the process of understanding must in some way be a mental process. We need to think about the word 'understanding' not in relation to what we assume it describes (the mental process) but in terms of the way it is used in the language; we need to separate the sign from the signified, the word from what it is thought to represent.

When someone says that they have 'understood x' this does not mean that they are laying claim to some internal, private piece of mental adjustment which has taken place in relation to x. The *word* 'understanding' only makes sense in public contexts. This becomes clear when we ask how we know that someone has 'understood x' because we can only properly answer that question by observing how they act and by listening to what they say. It would be possible in theory to test that understanding in some way, in a variety of contexts, by observing their behaviour or by asking questions. If someone says that they have understood that Dublin is the capital of Eire we would have no reason to doubt their claim unless in answer to the same question they now answer 'Galway' or if when asked the capital of England they again answer Dublin. If they fail those tests it would be difficult to see what 'understanding x' could possibly mean. The word gains its meaning not by a sudden mental event called 'understanding' but by what occurs before and after the particular moment in time when the claim to understanding is made.

It might be thought that in this view of understanding it is impossible really to say of someone that they have understood anything because theoretically the public tests could go on for ever. But that is precisely the point. It changes our view of understanding as 'an all or nothing affair' or as a particular event in time. This has implications both for what education entails and how assessment might be conceived. It means we can view education as a constant process of refining and deepening, seeing things from new angles, making fresh connections; no wonder drama practitioners had difficulty in pinning down the precise understanding which derived from a particular drama (see Chapter 1). Bruner's concept of a spiral curriculum is sometimes reduced to something similar to conducting revision sessions on topics previously studied. On this view of understanding however the concept of 'spiral curriculum' is much more fundamental. The importance of the analysis for assessment is to recognise that the 'rough edges' involved in making judgements are not an imperfection but an essential element of the process. To say about anyone that they have understood something, that they have acquired a particular skill or piece of knowledge can only ever be an approximate claim.

Previous philosophers had assumed that when we engage in such supposed mental activities as 'understanding', 'perceiving', 'imagining' there must be some sort of inner mental content which serves as their object. It is as if we could find the true, essential meaning of those words by looking inside someone, instead of examining how we use the words in our everyday life. We can point to someone walking and say 'this is walking' but we cannot do the same with the word 'thinking' and convey anything significant about what the word means.

> While we sometimes call it 'thinking' to accompany a sentence by a mental process, that accompaniment is not what we mean by a 'thought'. – Say a sentence and think it; say it with understanding. – And now do not say it, and just do what you accompanied it with when you said it with understanding!
>
> (Wittgenstein 1953:332).

Notice that Wittgenstein is not saying here that we are not able to say something and not understand what we are saying. The whole point of the imaginary imitation of the stool pigeon lesson is that the pupils would be drilled to imitate actions and mouth words without understanding. It is the understanding which cannot be abstracted from the context in which it finds expression.

The superficial grammar of our language seduces us into assuming that words like 'thinking' and 'understanding' refer to something going on inside us instead of pointing to patterns in our life. We speak of thoughts 'crossing one's mind' or of 'grasping the gist of what someone is saying' as if these words refer to something going on inside. But the words hold us captive. It is the circumstances which determine the legitimacy of the use of words like 'thinking' and 'understanding' (ibid:155).

> We are trying to get hold of the mental process of understanding which seems to be hidden behind those coarser and therefore more readily visible accompaniments. But we do not succeed; or, rather, it does not get us far as a real attempt.
>
> (ibid:153)

These insights have important consequences for drama and for arts education in general. If such activities as 'understanding', 'appreciating' and 'imagining' are wrongly thought to be essentially internal and hidden then this leads us in completely the wrong direction. The consequence is that we escape from any responsibility for what happens on the outside, so to speak; we are freed from any real accountability and responsibility in our teaching. Thus free, unstructured, 'creative' expression is legitimised by virtue of the benefits which are going on in the 'inner self'. Because these are by definition mysterious and hidden there are no real criteria for judging the efficacy of the educational process within the arts; it becomes simply a matter of blind faith. It makes no sense to say that the purpose of drama is to develop 'understanding' if by that we mean the development of some private, inner capacity.

The case against the inner self is reinforced by Wittgenstein's argument against the possibility of a private language. A private language is one whose words 'refer to what can only be known to the person speaking: to his immediate private sensations'(1953:243). Could we, he asks

> imagine a language in which a person could write down or give vocal expression to his inner experiences – his feelings, moods and the rest – for his private use? Well, can't we do so in our ordinary language? But that is not what I mean. The individual words of this language are to refer to what can only be known to the person speaking; to his immediate private sensations. So another person cannot understand the language.   (p.243)

Such a language would only be possible if words acquire meaning simply by being linked to private experiences. One of the objections to the possibility of a private language is that there would be no guarantee of consistency in using the language. In order for that to happen criteria of correctness or rules are required which arise in contexts of agreement between people. The argument rests on the fact that language has meaning largely in external public contexts; in Wittgenstein's terms a considerable degree of 'stage-setting' is required when naming of a sensation takes place. If someone claims to report something as being 'true' that can only happen if there is some means of establishing independent criteria.

Returning to the application of these arguments to drama and art, it becomes apparent that any educational argument in favour of private, individualistic experiences suffers because of an inability even to talk about what is going on. For that to happen we need agreement in shared, communal contexts which accords with a contemporary emphasis on the social and cultural aspects of drama. To make sense of language which is applied to the outcomes of drama it has to be linked to behavioural criteria. This is important when it comes to questions of assessment and evaluation, for we can only properly judge what we can see.

Wittgenstein effectively abolished the notion of a metaphysically private self and his arguments seem to support Hornbrook's emphasis on demonstrably public products. However, we have in the process seemed to have arrived at a highly positivistic, behavioural position which as art educators is hardly the place we would want to be. This, however, is precisely the place to which drama educators have been pushed by the inexorable logic of arguments against dualism. Surely, however, art is above all else about the human inner life and inner processes? How do we resolve the peculiar *reductio ad absurdum* to which the logical argument seems to have taken us? Logic and intuition seem to point in different directions. If we return to the examples of the two drama lessons (the 'real' and the replicated) we judge each lesson by the external behaviour of the participants. We have no method in the basis of the discussion so far from distinguishing the 'real' lesson from the one in which the pupils' responses were mindlessly drilled.

The important point about Wittgenstein's writing is that it is essentially focused on language. This is a point that is often missed in discussions about 'inner processes' in relation to drama and art. His argument has largely to do with the grammar of the way we use words rather than a reductive, behavioural account of how we function as human beings. An 'inner process' he says 'stands in need of outward criteria' but that is not the same as saying that the concept of an inner process makes no sense at all. Nor does it mean that in the context of education we have to avoid making reference to the inner life; on the contrary the impact of Wittgenstein's philosophy is precisely to liberate us to focus on inner processes in our teaching, without necessarily being accused of mysticism, of chasing 'ghosts' of subscribing to forms of dualism.

The same analysis of language which abolished the inner self also abolishes the purely external, objectified physical world. Whereas before Wittgenstein a statement like that might have sounded like a dubious claim to idealism (or a contemporary piece of pseudo postmodernism) we can now see it as statement about the way language works. Since Descartes, epistemological explanations aimed at explaining how it is that we know what we know have puzzled and eluded philosophers. Wittgenstein's approach is to show that the sceptic's doubt about the existence of an external world is operating within a different language game. The attempt to establish the kind of knowledge and certainty which the philosophical sceptic seeks is trying to look *behind* our normal uses of the words 'knowledge' and 'certainty' but it is an illusion to think that there is anything there (Wittgenstein 1969:19). 'Doubting the existence of the external world does not mean for example doubting the existence of a planet which later observations proved to exist' (ibid:20). Doubts about the existence of material objects do not make any difference in practice (ibid:120). We do not have to choose between a rigorous objectivity or spurious subjectivity. What we have instead is a more integrated view of 'inner' and 'outer' dimensions of experience.

'Thinking', 'understanding, 'perceiving', 'responding', 'feeling' are part of the factual world but because they are not locked away and private they can now have more significant influence on the way we think about education. The traditional philosophical concept of the inner self rendered it mysterious and hidden such that it did not actually have any direct effect on teaching. But abolishing any reference to the inner life is in danger of throwing the baby out with the bath water which is precisely what we have to guard against in drama teaching. The blind faith in 'public products', irrespective of how these are experienced by pupils, arises precisely for that reason.

If we return to the example of the Heathcote lesson and ask whether it matters that we cannot distinguish between the 'real' and the 'replicated' product the answer has to be that it all depends. If we are watching the 'performance' as an audience for our own edification and insight it hardly matters because what we see in both cases will be identical. However, if we are interested in the educational benefits for the pupils this suggests that their degree of understanding and engagement does matter. But we do not distinguish the 'real' from the 'replicated' experience by looking inside the pupils. This is the understandable mistake made by many writers on drama because without resorting to the internal there seems to be no criterion for distinguishing one type of experience from another.

Wittgenstein was not so much denying the existence of inner states but pointing out that the way in which the language we use, which appears to describe inner states, gets its meaning is by virtue of the contexts in which people act. To borrow helpful terminology used by McGinn (1997:67) we need to direct our attention away from what *accompanies* particular activities in drama towards the *context* or circumstances in which the drama takes place.

It is by examining the overall context that we can comment on the quality of the experience in the 'stool pigeon' examples. Only then can we establish that in the 'real' case the pupils were involved in the planning, understood the context and had some ownership of what was going on. We are entitled to conclude that they had an appropriate level of feeling in the final 'performance' but we make this judgement only by examining the external process and patterns of behaviour. That is why it is inappropriate in drama teaching as discussed in the previous chapter to separate means from ends, for they are inextricably linked. To say that a scheme of work should contain melodrama, medieval theatre, etc., in the course of a drama curriculum tells us nothing unless we know what that means in practice, unless we know the context and circumstances in which these activities are embedded.

Assessing drama

The above discussion suggests that assessment of drama is likely to require strategies which provide some insight into process as well as product. In other words if an assessor observes pupils enacting a scene from a play or performing a devised piece based on an improvisation this will be far more informative if it is accompanied by some insight into either the prior preparation and planning or into the way pupils respond to what they or others have created. 'Performing' is usually identified as a separate attainment for drama and the wisdom of this tradition will be challenged. Trying to assess 'performing' on its own without some relationship to process will yield very little information about a pupil's understanding. Performing is both 'everything' and 'nothing' (to adapt an enigmatic phrase from Wittgenstein).

In reality an assessor may be able make judgements about participants' understanding, involvement, depth of feeling without necessarily being aware of all the work which preceded a particular project. The important point is those opinions are based on inferences about context and they are not claims to knowledge about internal states. Another consequence of the preceding discussion is that we do not have to disinfect the language we use in relation to assessment in the arts in order to avoid words which have subjective overtones.

It was suggested in Chapter 1 that it is part of the tradition of drama in education to celebrate the achievements of the teacher rather than the pupils. The stool pigeon lesson taught by Dorothy Heathcote was celebrated not because the pupils were thought to be outstanding at drama but because this was an example of excellent teaching. It is unlikely that the pupils had much previous experience of drama yet within the space of a few days they produced work of very high quality. This tradition is still found in accounts of process drama where the artistry of the teacher is valued rather more than that of the participants. Although contemporary accounts of assessment in drama tend to focus more on what the pupils are creating and achieving, the teaching process clearly requires teacher support or 'scaffolding'. This makes the assessment process complex because it is sometimes difficult to distinguish pupils' achievements from those of the teacher. Another difficulty with assessment is that drama is primarily a social activity. It is normally an individual's progress which needs to be reported and it is not always easy to disentangle this from a group activity. A pupil's performance or contribution in drama is often context specific; what they contribute and achieve may depend on the particular topic which is the subject of the drama.

Simons (2000:23) has pointed out another problem with assessment in drama. The content of the lesson often 'deviates from the plan because of spontaneous input from the students and on-the-spot changes in direction by the teacher'. It is important therefore that 'the planned assessment tasks need to be fairly flexible'. All of these issues add to the complexity of the task of assessing pupils in drama.

Several publications in recent years provide practical guidance for departments faced with the challenge of formulating an assessment policy. The Arts Council publication *Drama in Schools* specified three attainment targets, described in the report as 'activities': making, performing, responding. A similar framework was used by Hornbrook (1991:141) which adopted a National Curriculum structure of attainment targets and statements of attainment for the end of key stages. For example under 'making' which is described as 'the development of students' ability to manipulate dramatic form in order to interpret and express ideas', pupils at the end of Key Stage 2 (age 11) will be expected to: 'contribute imaginatively, as a member of a group, to the making of a rehearsed dramatic scene: show in their play making that they can structure coherent dramatic narratives; incorporate a choice of dramatic techniques and conventions in their play making; read familiar playscripts and understand how stage directions are used; demonstrate an understanding of how dramatic action is framed in performance'.

The National Drama Secondary Drama Teacher's Handbook (1998) provides a variety of advice on such topics as: the use of evidence to support assessment; the frequency of assessments; the types of strategies which can be used. The publication includes an example of a pre-printed sheet given to each student at the start of each module outlining the aims and the assessment criteria. For example, in a unit on poetry in drama the pupils are told they will be assessed on:

- use of sounds and movement (Making Drama)
- your ideas about the people (Making Drama)
- how you communicate your ideas to an audience (Performing Drama)
- your ideas during the process of working and end-product drama (Responding to drama).

An example of a pupil profile is also provided which is used to record the teacher's assessment of individual students against the following criteria: organisation, cooperation, group work; listening; ability to adopt a role, response to play texts; use of language, body language, performance, responding and evaluating. Each of these areas is broken down into five further criteria. For example 'response to play texts' is described in terms of the following areas: 'gives imaginative ideas, interprets role and situation, experiments with alternative viewpoints, understands and communicates themes, shows an awareness of performance values'. The assessment seems complex described in this way but all of the criteria fit easily into a grid on one A4 sheet.

Assessing Drama (Clark and Goode 1999) describes in its first chapter the key official documents which have had a bearing on assessment in the arts. The publication as a whole illustrates well the particular challenge drama faces in coping with assessment. For example, the chapter on primary drama suggests some 28 possible areas of focus for assessment under various headings (drama as a subject: the art form; drama as a context for speaking and listening; drama as a context for reading and writing; drama to support learning in other subjects) illustrating the potential complexity of the process. A framework for assessment is provided under three headings: personal, social and expressive skills; conceptual learning (both cognitive and affective); understanding and working with dramatic form. These headings and the suggestions provide a starting point for teachers seeking to work out an assessment scheme: 'for these criteria to become effective the individual teacher will need to organise them into an established set or rubric which outlines the range of performance levels expected in the demonstration of an outcome and tells the teacher exactly what they should be looking for when determining an individual student's performance' (ibid:73). The list of suggestions for methods of assessment is helpful and again illustrates the potential complexity of the process: observation, narrative accounts, audio/video taping, photography, seminar presentation, performance, creative reflection, talk, questionnaires, making a dossier, self-assessment, peer-assessment, workshop practice.

Neelands (1998) *Beginning Drama 11–14*, in common with many recent publications, also acknowledges the importance of making, performing and responding in assessing drama. The aims and objectives for a drama course at Key Stage 3 include learning about genres and technique, working as a group member, and watching and evaluating performance. The book provides very specific details of progression through seven levels under the headings of 'dramatic action', 'adopting role' and 'theatre making'. The section on assessment provides a suggested scheme for evaluating standards in drama at Key Stage 3 based on the previous model. The author (ibid:22) highlights the fact that different schools may value drama for different reasons and this will be reflected in the assessment arrangements.

> In some schools assessment may focus on the personal and interpersonal behaviour of students. In others the assessment of drama may be subsumed into the assessment of English: the contribution that drama makes to the development of linguistic and literacy skills and knowledge. In schools that view KS3 drama as a foundation and recruiting ground for KS4, assessment might focus on students' preparedness for further studies in drama leading to a qualification. The demands for accountability in drama may also vary from school to school according to the value that drama is given in the curriculum: some schools may require and take note of detailed assessments in drama; in others there may be little point in providing any detail beyond an assessment of a student's level of confidence and willingness to work with others in an effective way.

Clark and Short (1999) identify three 'key areas essential to the teaching and learning of drama' as 'dramatic form', 'performance and expressive skills', and 'communication and response'. Each of these areas is broken down into strands. For example dramatic form contains five strands: plot/script, techniques, role/risk and play, genre, symbolism, each of which in turn has descriptors related to six levels. The scheme seeks specifically to encompass aspects of process and performance reflecting the particular theoretical orientation of its authors.

Kempe and Ashwell (2000) identify three 'areas of activity' (crea performing, responding) each of which is broken down into four strands which turn has eight levels (plus 'exceptional performance'). The 'progression chart' which results is intended to help teachers with a means of plotting the knowledge, skills and understanding being acquired by the students (ibid:43). The authors also suggested an approach to 'baseline assessment' whereby a project on small group play making is used to assess pupils at three different levels (working towards, working at the level, working above) on a variety of criteria.

These publications represent a sample of the different suggestions available to support teachers faced with the task of planning a scheme for assessment. They are summarised in Table 4.1. Rather than attempt to create another framework to add to the burgeoning list, the aim here will be to be explore some of the tensions and difficulties involved in creating schemes of this kind.

Even from the very brief summary given in Table 4.1 the sheer complexity of the process of assessing drama is striking. One of the tensions at the heart of any assessment process is that between reliability and validity. Reliable forms of assessment are needed in order to compare pupils' levels of achievement fairly. Reliability has to do with the degree to which the form of assessment is likely to yield the same results if repeated on different occasions and judged by different people. A multiple choice test asking pupils to identify the writers of different plays will be very reliable (using the term purely in a technical sense) but it is unlikely to be considered a very appropriate method of assessing drama. Forms of assessment may be reliable but that does not mean that they are valid. The traditional definition of validity is 'the extent to which a test measures what it was designed to measure' (Stobart and Gipps 1990:40). The complexity of schemes for assessing drama derive in part from the desire of their authors to create forms of assessment which are valid, which represent the subject adequately. Validity and reliability, however, tend to pull in different directions. A teacher may have devised a complex system for evaluating work in drama across a range of different strands and using a variety of different methods of recording work but when challenged may find it difficult to justify a particular grade in comparison to that given to another pupil. The accumulation of extensive evidence in the form of records, self-evaluations, photographs, audio tapes will not necessarily help because it may be difficult to compare one portfolio to another.

Drama is inevitably influenced by the prevailing educational climate which tends to value summative (making judgements at specific times) over formative assessment (which is associated more with feedback). Providing pupils with specific feedback in relation to their work in drama has not been a feature of much of the writing about drama over the years. Analysis of lessons tended to focus on how the teacher might have improved the teaching rather than how well the pupils responded to what they were asked to do. Providing feedback was implicitly

	Main 'attainment targets'	Example of one 'attainment target' broken down into individual statements
	• making • performing • responding	Performing. At the end of Key Stage 2 pupils should be able to: invent and sustain interesting and convincing roles in a drama; adapt voice and movement to the demands of a chosen role or character; perform confidently as a member of a group to peers and selected adults; carry out appropriate 'backstage' tasks during a performance.
Neelands (1998)	• making • performing • responding	'Responding' described in seven levels (first three are given here): understanding relationship between 'next action' and the narrative sequence; understanding the causal relationship between actions taken; recognising the action as being 'context specific'.
Clark and Goode (1999)	• personal, social and expressive skills • conceptual learning (both cognitive and affective) • understanding and working with dramatic form	Criteria for conceptual learning: level of identification with the theme; ability to extend the ideas within the theme; ability to reflect on the meanings created in the drama during and after the experience.
Clark and Short (1999)	• dramatic form • performance and expressive skills • communication and response	Each target has five strands: e.g. 'dramatic form': plots/scripts, techniques, role/risk and play, genre, symbolism. Each strand has six levels.
Kempe and Ashwell (2000)	• creating • performing • responding	Each target has four strands: e.g. performing: working supportively with others in performance; interpreting narrative and portraying character in performance; manipulating the different signs through which drama communicates meaning; realising a range of genres, styles and forms for different purposes and addressing different audiences. Each strand has eight levels.

associated with 'coaching' and 'directing' and with placing an undue emphasis on 'external' features of the work. In order to provide a valid assessment of drama there is a temptation to want to make the assessment as wide-ranging as possible. This raises the spectre of pupils and teachers constantly collecting evidence in order to inform a summative assessment process but not necessarily integrating these into the teaching and learning process.

The complexity of some of the schemes identified here suggests a need to distinguish programmes of study from attainment targets. This terminology was introduced as part of the National Curriculum framework to distinguish between the content of the syllabus and the focus for assessment. It is a useful distinction because it recognises that assessment, no matter how complex, can only ever be based on a *selection* of what a broad and balanced drama syllabus will look like. If the assessment scheme seeks to include everything which is considered important it may become difficult to lay claim to any reliability. It may also become so complex that the process of filling in details for every pupil in a class of 30 will become unmanageable.

Another issue related to the development of assessment schemes is the tacit belief in the transparency of language. This is the assumption that the more detailed the identification of targets, levels and strands, the more there will be a common focus and shared understanding by those using the scheme. But of course language is not that transparent; which can simply be illustrated by taking a fairly arbitrary sample of statements and asking the question 'what do they mean?': 'show awareness of self in drama', 'realising the dramatic potential of the visual and written text', 'maintain narrative consistency within a dramatic improvisation', 'responding to and using elements of form'. For example it is difficult to imagine anyone taking part in drama without 'responding to and using elements of form'. Key questions immediately come to mind such as 'to what degree?' (better than last time or last year?) and 'in what way?'. The point is not to disparage the work of writers who have worked on assessment schemes but to recognise that the language contained within them will only have real meaning when exemplified through practice. Moderation meetings for GCSE provide the type of sharing of interpretation which needs to be extended to other phases if assessment in drama can make any claim to reliability.

A key tension underlying the assessment process of drama is the danger of reducing it merely to an evaluation of skills and reducing attention to the importance of meaning and content. Clark and Goode's scheme for example includes 'conceptual learning both cognitive and affective' as one of the areas of assessment (1999:73). Assessment of learning in relation to content as discussed in Chapter 1 has been a central problem for drama in education. Here, however, Clark and Goode refer not so much to describing the precise learning in relation to the theme in propositions (e.g. 'that bullies are often insecure people') but the responsiveness of pupils to content, e.g. 'ability to extend the ideas within a theme'. This is a helpful distinction. As suggested in Chapter 1 the importance of meaning and content in relation to drama is extremely important. It is not enough for pupils for example to be able 'demonstrate the use of a wide variety of dramatic forms and techniques' but to do so in a way which 'explores and communicates ideas with increasing depth and complexity'. The importance of content however can be acknowledged in a summary statement of the attainment target rather than repeated at each level. For example Hornbrook's definition of making: 'the development of students' ability to manipulate dramatic form in order to interpret and manipulate ideas' could be interpreted as containing an implicit recognition of the importance of content or could be developed to make that aspect more explicit: 'the development of students' ability to manipulate dramatic form in order to interpret and express ideas and to probe their depth and meaning'. The specific language, however, is less important than its interpretation in practice.

On the basis of the theoretical discussion in this chapter and given the recent history of the subject, it is time to abandon the distinction between 'performing' and 'making' in assessment of drama. The emphasis on the importance of context and process in judging what has previously been thought of as 'internal' dimensions of experience compels this view. This is not to suggest that performance is not an important part of drama; on the contrary, communicating and performing can almost be described as defining elements of the genre. However, the distinction between 'making' and 'performing' in assessment implies that a performance can be judged irrespective of any relationship to context. As Bolton (1999:41) asks, 'If a pupil tries out an idea in action, is that to be seen as "making" or "performing"?' To preserve the distinction is in danger of privileging slick forms of 'theatricality' at the expense of 'understanding', 'authenticity' and 'feeling'.

To suggest abandoning 'performance' as an attainment target 12 years ago (the introduction of the National Curriculum in England) would have been interpreted as an argument against performance *per se*, and an implicit argument against audiences, scripts, responding to drama (all the elements of which were somewhat neglected in the extremes of drama in education practice in the 1970s). But that is far from being the case. Abandoning performing as a separate attainment target is paradoxically to raise its status, to recognise its central importance in almost every drama activity which is undertaken. But it is also to abandon the notion that performing can be separated out and assessed separately. That is why performance is both 'everything' and 'nothing'. Statements which are listed under 'making' in the various schemes are invariably demonstrated in some aspect of performance, e.g. 'demonstrate an understanding of how dramatic action is framed in performance', 'experiment with unorthodox dramatic approaches to material to produce dramas which are thought-provoking and original'.

There are pragmatic as well as theoretical reasons for fusing 'making' and 'performing'. The reduction in attainment targets reduces the complexity of the assessment process. For younger primary age pupils it is particularly difficult to sustain the distinction. This was recognised by Hornbrook (1991) when he suggested that 'teachers may wish to pull the first two attainment targets – Making and Performing – into one and assess work under a single Profile Component – Production'. The National Curriculum arts project (NCC 1990) identified 'making' and 'appraising' as two areas of assessment in the arts. Continuity and progression will be better served by having a consistent framework through the key stages.

This chapter will not conclude with an alternative assessment scheme based on just two attainment targets. In the absence of a national framework for drama the work of Clark and Short (1999) illustrates the value of devising assessment schemes at a local level. The suggestions which have been published provide ample support for teachers engaged in this process. For example the book by Kempe and Ashwell (2000) provides access to a web site so that their grid for tracking progression can be downloaded and adapted to local needs. What is needed is not so much the proliferation of more schemes but moderation of teacher judgements which at present is largely confined to assessment at GCSE.

Another reason for not rushing to write an alternative assessment scheme is that the discussion is far from complete. 'Making' and 'responding' are invariably found in schemes for assessing drama but there are also dangers in treating those elements entirely separately. The relationship between 'making' and 'responding' will be discussed in more detail in the next chapter.

CHAPTER 5

Progression in drama: making and responding

A drama session is in progress, using Alfred Noyes' poem *The Highwayman* as its central focus. The participants read the first section and work in small groups to prepare three still images each depicting an everyday scene involving one of the three characters (the ostler working in the stable, Bess working in the inn, the highwayman on the road). These are presented so that the rest of the participants can guess which character is being represented. The groups now devise a still image which involves all three characters together to show their understanding of the poem. Relevant lines are read aloud to accompany the presentations. As the group observe and respond to the images, the teacher asks speculative questions: Does Bess know that the ostler loves her? Does the landlord know that Bess is seeing the highwayman? We are not told anything about Bess's mother – what might have happened to her? What does the ostler think of the highwayman? How does the highwayman treat the ostler?

The group try to predict what will happen in the poem before they read the next two sections in which they learn that Bess dies in her attempt to save the highwayman from an ambush set by the king's men. He in turn dies while seeking to avenge her death. As the group read, they create sounds to accompany the words (e.g. the horses hooves on the cobbles, the clash of the window). Their next task is to question the teacher in role as the ostler about his actions, trying to establish whether he betrayed the highwayman and, if so, what were his motives. The group now imagine it is a week or so after the events described in the poem and the commanding officer has sent two investigators back to the inn to find out what happened to Bess. Some historical information is introduced: highwaymen often used coaching inns as a refuge when they were being pursued; they often bribed the innkeeper to keep quiet about their presence; there have been some examples of wealthy and well-known people who became highwaymen when they ran into debt; highwaymen frequently wore masks so they could not be identified. In groups of four or five the pupils plan and enact their own investigations trying to establish the truth of what happened to Bess. Although on the surface this is an exercise in uncovering the true facts, the underlying theme relates to the father's motivation, parental responsibility, disloyalty and guilt.

Elsewhere a drama session is being taught based on an adapted version of the story of the three little pigs in which the wolf protests his innocence and declares that knocking the houses down was an accident. The participants alternate their roles as lawyers defending the wolf and the community of pigs who spread malicious gossip and attempt to blacken his name. In one of the drama activities small groups prepare a TV broadcast aimed at rebuilding the wolf's image in the community.

These two lessons are highly truncated versions of more extended projects, the full versions of which can be read in Fleming (2000) and Taylor (2000). They have been described here without giving any indication of the groups for which the projects were designed. In fact, the second session has, according to Taylor, 'been taught with primary, secondary and higher education students' (ibid:8). The Highwayman drama was originally conducted with a Year 5 (age 10) but it could just as easily be used with younger or older pupils. I have used it in practical sessions with teachers as a project for them to adapt for their own classes. While doing so I have recognised that they have derived value from the work at their own level.

These two drama sessions raise questions about the issue of progression in drama. The significant factor is not so much that the projects can be easily used with different age groups (ranging from primary to higher education) but the related implication that the different groups may have very different past experiences of drama. If, as suggested in the previous chapter, drama teachers can produce work of impressive quality with a class irrespective of the pupils' previous experience in the subject, how do we make sense of the notion that a drama syllabus or scheme of work should be structured according to some underlying principle of progression? This issue clearly relates very closely to that of assessment but it has wider implications: progression is also important in order to provide a coherent curriculum and for the pupils themselves to have a sense of achievement and direction.

We need not be surprised that the same content and tasks can be used with different groups. After all, A *Midsummer Night's Dream* appears in the primary school or university seminar. Although the projects described above appear to use material which is more normally associated with younger classes, the content has wider appeal. The ironic reversal in the Sciezska version of the three pigs story on which the drama is based widens the appeal for older participants. *The Highwayman* is a popular poem with teachers of primary age pupils because of its very strong stylistic features although some of its content is more adult.

As suggested, what is more surprising is not that the content and tasks can be used with a wide range of age groups but that the prior knowledge, skill and understanding in drama appears to be of minimal relevance to the success of the project. In many of the lessons drawn from the tradition of drama in education the learning (and by implication the teaching) did not appear to be cumulative in its nature. In process drama the participants tend to move from one rich experience to another but there is often little sense of building on what went before. It is not necessary to rush to criticism over that fact, despite the obsession in current educational discourse with issues of continuity and progression. After all we do not in our everyday lives seek to structure our experiences of art: as if we cannot allow ourselves to watch a performance of *Hamlet* without first serving an apprenticeship watching miracle plays. It could be argued that the proof of the drama is in the teaching; if 'process drama' lessons are successful without the imposition of an artificial framework of progression why concede to what might be conceived as current educational fashion? Is there not a danger in placing too much emphasis on external structures rather than on the quality of the experience of the participants (see Chapter 2)? In order to throw some extra light on these questions it will be helpful to distinguish two uses of 'progression'.

Progression

Although progression has been more to the fore in discussions about drama teaching in recent years, it was not ignored by earlier writers. Slade who is invariably characterised as being anti theatre, saw performance in front of an audience as coming at the end of a process of natural development in drama. He based his views largely on his own informal observations of children, noticing that they tend to group themselves in particular physical shapes during their play which reflected their natural inclination to a particular form of drama. He described the successive stages as: closed circle, gang circle, running circle, leading eventually to the proscenium arch.

Bolton (1998:124) has pointed out the overlap in Slade's theorising between psychological and theatrical explanations.

> Any observation he makes about the psychology or sociology of child behaviour, therefore, tends to be finally expressed by Slade in artistic terms. When he writes for example of young children's typical satisfaction in 'banging things', Slade interprets such experimentation as the development of 'rhythm and climax'. Thus a *psychological* phenomenon, 'satisfaction from banging' is seen as having an *aesthetic* potential.

Courtney writing in the 1960s identified stages of dramatic education which also saw theatre (which was conceived in traditional terms as performance before an audience) as being more appropriate for older pupils. The stages were very straightforward: primary (5–11 years) dramatic play; secondary (11–18 years) dramatic play mingling with 'theatre'; tertiary (18+ years) 'theatre' based on dramatic play.

Slade in particular, as has been well documented, was very much influenced by a Rousseauesque concept of natural development in education. He was concerned to minimise the intervention of the teacher and allow pupils to progress and learn at their own pace. We could describe his and Courtney's account of progression as *descriptive* (providing an account of how it is that pupils develop in drama).

Descriptive accounts of progression derive in part from the close association of 'drama' with 'play'. For Slade the terms were largely synonymous because he saw the dramatic playing of young children as an art form in its own right. Later, with the development of 'drama in education', the term 'play' became one of disparagement; pupils who were not involved in the drama at an appropriate level of depth and seriousness were merely 'wallowing in meaningless playing' (Bolton 1979:29). Davis and Lawrence (1986:viii) described the move away from make-believe play which was once conceived as the 'fundamental model and building block in educational drama' because it had 'too strong an emphasis on direct experiencing'. This movement away from dramatic playing continued in the 1990s with exponents looking less to psychological theories of child play and more to writers on theatre and semiotics for the theoretical underpinning for their work. The change of emphasis can be summarised as a move from a 'personal' to a more 'cultural' justification for drama or an emphasis on 'culture' as opposed to 'nature'.

Descriptive accounts of progression then recognise that drama has its origins in the dramatic play of the young child. The emphasis is rather more on spontaneity and natural development, and much less on conscious construction of meaning. Progression is likely to be judged in terms of maturity rather than the growth which comes about as a result of external intervention. There are parallels with developmental theories in psychology which seek to identify the stages through which children pass as part of their natural development. The implications for teaching are significant because, on this view, an attempt to introduce tasks prematurely before children are ready are likely to be unsuccessful. For example children who are still at the stage of concrete operations will not be able to cope with demands of more conceptual thinking. Although researchers like Donaldson (1978) have demonstrated the importance of context in determining response to tasks, the basic developmental principle remains the same.

More contemporary accounts of progression in drama can be described as *prescriptive*. These seek to specify the knowledge and skills which pupils should be taught in sequence rather than attempt to describe natural stages of development. The term 'prescriptive' is not being used here in a negative sense to imply 'authoritarian insistence' but to contrast with developmental accounts. Like so many conceptual distinctions discussed in this book, the difference between the two uses of 'progression' tend to overlap. Developmental theories of progression in drama do not assume that pupils left entirely to their own devices will move through the appropriate stages; Slade (1954:131) saw the teacher as a kindly gentle guide, avoiding 'too many fussy, unnecessary suggestions'. Prescriptive accounts of progression need to have a descriptive element to them; all such frameworks need to be bounded by some notion of what is possible at particular ages. That this is obvious becomes clear if we simply think about the teaching of reading: without a realistic descriptive element to accounts of progression in reading there would nothing to stop the imposition of Dostoevesky in the reception class.

Two recent publications include frameworks for describing progression. Both were referred to in the previous chapter because accounts of progression have important implications for assessment. Kempe and Ashwell (2000:36) provide an example of a 'progression chart' to be used as a guide for teachers when 'plotting and monitoring' the work that students do in drama within a scheme of work. Twelve strands within three areas (creating, performing, responding) provide a means for checking that pupils have a 'breadth and balance of experience'. The eight levels (plus exceptional performance) which are related to each strand provide a means for monitoring progression in a particular aspect of drama. Thus within one of the creating strands, 'working supportively and creatively with others', the progression works from level one ('plan an imaginative play area with others') to level eight ('solve problems in the devising process by offering solutions which demonstrate awareness of the skills of the group'). The framework which is provided for schools to adapt as they see fit draws on drama requirements in the National Curriculum, National Literacy Strategy, GCSE syllabuses and OFSTED guidance (ibid:37).

Neelands (1998:15) describes progresssion in drama at Key Stage 3 through seven levels in relation to making/performing and responding. In the making/performing category pupils move from 'proposing next action in a narrative sequence' (level one) to 'directing and executing a sequence of practised actions to create a sustained dramatic statement' (level seven). Descriptions are also given in relation to role development and progression in theatre-making. One characteristic of the table which summarises progression from Key Stage 3 to 4 in eight different categories is the pupils' increasing independence from the teacher. There is a progression from 'the simple unreflexive realism of younger students' drama making, in which the teacher is very much at the centre of a class's work', to 'students being given and taking increasing responsibility for their own group work with the teacher working in the margins, guiding, managing, monitoring and assessing the work of the groups' (ibid:19). The categories are also intended to reflect what the author describes as 'aesthetic progression' with a movement from naturalism to postnaturalist theatre movements.

The emphasis on the increasing independence of the pupils in relation to different aspects of drama work is a departure from traditional drama in education practice and much process drama in which the teacher's role in structuring the drama, challenging pupils' thinking and creating an appropriate level of feeling is paramount. In developmental accounts of progression the teacher's role tends to be minimised because progression was thought to happen naturally. One of the implications of a more descriptive account is to raise questions about the nature of teaching in drama. Whereas the concept of 'learning' in drama has had much analysis and discussion, the concept of 'teaching' has had rather less attention and will be considered here in relation to the concept of 'making'.

Making

Much discussion in drama has centred on the distinction between 'learning in' (the acquisition of knowledge and skills specifically related to drama) and 'learning through' (knowledge and understanding related to the content or theme). Many writers now accept that an approach to the subject based on one or other conception of learning is far too limited. The view expressed by Bowell and Heap (2001:124) (who are committed to process drama and the importance of content) is not untypical.

> While assessment of pupils' progress in their understanding, of, say, conservation issues, evolution or the Australian gold rush, or of their ability to work as team members or to problem-solve, is absolutely appropriate and desirable, assessing the achievements *only* which are content led or concerned with personal and social development will *not* provide the teacher with an insight into the progress her pupils are making *in drama*.

The dichotomy between 'learning through' and 'learning in' can be related to the question of what 'teaching drama' entails. As Bolton pointed out in 1979, writing about his experiences prior to the development of drama in education, it was not customary to speak about 'teaching drama'.

> When I was a young teacher colleagues might out of interest have asked me occasionally what I was doing with a particular class of children in drama, but nobody as far as I can remember actually asked me what I was *teaching* them ... learning and teaching were all right for other subjects, but in drama one just thought and talked about what one was *doing*.   (Bolton 1999:30)

Bolton sought to give meaning to the concept of 'teaching drama' by focusing on content. In his second book (1984:151) in which he saw drama as an effective way of developing 'common understanding through the exercise of basic mental powers' a central role of the teacher was to look for 'opportunities to break the perceptions and conceptions of his pupils' (ibid:157). 'Teaching drama' meant seeking ways to develop pupils' understanding. What 'teaching drama' might mean in relation to development of ability *in* drama tended to be given rather less attention by writers for a number of reasons. Drama was seen as a 'natural' activity. One of its perceived strengths in education was that participants could engage in making drama without any training in acting or other theatre skills. This meant that advocates of drama in education were free to concentrate on content. 'Teaching drama' was associated in people's minds with narrow ideas about coaching, training and participating in exercises with little sense of purpose. Teaching drama skills was associated with a lack of authenticity; a tradition from which drama in education had departed.

Progressive theories of education tended to associate 'teaching' with 'telling' or simple transmission. One aspect of the reaction against traditional, authoritarian views was to play down the concept of 'teaching' in favour of notions like 'facilitator' or 'creator of learning contexts'. Conceptual philosophers who reacted against what they saw as extreme forms of child centred education formulated their criticisms in what appeared to be neutral forms of analysis. Teaching was often defined in terms of an 'intention to bring about learning' (Hirst 1974:105). The slogan of some progressives, 'we teach children not subjects', was challenged by the idea that teaching as a verb must have two accusatives, teaching x (subject matter) to y (a person). The challenge to progressive thinking was also captured in the quotation from Skinner which appeared in a frontspiece in *Perspectives on Plowden* (Peters 1969):

> The school of experience is not school at all, not because no one learns in it but because no one teaches. Teaching is the expedition of learning; a person who is taught learns more quickly that one who is not.

One of the questions implicit in the distinction between descriptive and prescriptive accounts of progression is to what degree drama is a natural activity which does not need teaching. Is it more like learning to speak or is it more like learning to write? The parallels with the teaching of language are illuminating. According to Pinker (1994:189) language is an instinct, written language is not. A 'language in use' approach, as the phrase suggests, took the view that language develops by its meaningful use in appropriate contexts. But this is a necessary rather than sufficient condition for the development of language, particularly in the case of reading and writing. Young children learn to speak as long as they are brought up in a social environment; in fact it would be almost impossible to stop them learning to speak as long as they are exposed to language. However some unhelpful polarities have been created when the same principle has been applied to other aspects of language use (phonics versus whole books). Pupils do not learn to write by being exposed to paper and pencils; they need more specific guidance than this (instruction, feedback, etc.). Pupils need more direct teaching than exponents of an extreme 'language in use' approach assumed although the principle that the creation of appropriate meaningful contexts is important still holds.

Language and drama are both to some degree 'natural activities'. In the case of drama this is reflected in descriptive accounts of progression in which the teacher's role is implicitly seen as providing contexts, motivating, setting and facilitating interesting tasks, advising, engaging interest and involvement. But in the case of both drama and language this has lead to an underestimation of what needs to be taught (i.e. instructed, demonstrated, explained and so on).

If we return to the examples of the lessons given at the beginning of this chapter we can look at some of the activities more closely in terms of this discussion of teaching. In the lesson based on *The Highwayman* the pupils are asked to conduct an investigation into the events at the inn and the actual description of the project indicates what specific teaching is required in order to help the success of that task. It is suggested that the teacher and a pupil first demonstrate what might be involved. One of the pupils is invited to take the part of the landlord who is questioned by the teacher in role as an investigator. The purpose of the demonstration is to help the pupils enact their own scenes. What is the landlord doing when the knock comes to the door? Does he welcome the investigator in straight away or is he reluctant at first? (Fleming 2000).

The questions direct the pupils to think about the framing devices which they might use prior to the beginning of the dialogue – do the landlord's actions relate in any way to his character or state of mind? By asking the pupils to consider how the landlord reacts to the investigator the pupils are being taught how to inject an element of tension and interest into the scene from the beginning.

The pupils are then asked to consider and share questions which might be put to the landlord. This part of the preparation is of course related to content but the pupils are being taught how to construct dialogue and how to adopt an appropriate tone.

> I realise you must still be distressed at the death of your daughter but do you mind answering some questions we would like to put to you?
> What mood were the soldiers in when they arrived at the inn?
> Could you show me exactly where they sat?
> Did you overhear any of their conversations?
> You say you remained upstairs in your room when the soldiers arrived – did you hear anything unusual?
> Could we go to the room in which Bess's body was found?
> You say that Bess spent quite a lot of time with the highwayman – could you tell me more about that please?
> Or…you say you left the inn before the soldiers and came back to find Bess dead. Were you not worried leaving her like that?

The pupils are advised that more interest and tension is created if the landlord is either concealing what happened or for some reason does not know himself. The same applies to the other characters who might be interviewed in the course of an investigation: people who were drinking in the inn that evening, the ostler, one of the soldiers. These do not just involve question and answer interviews but might involve varied actions, e.g. the investigators can be shown to various rooms which are critical to the investigation or they might search the inn. Pupils are here being taught that the meaning is conveyed not just by words but by actions. They are also advised that they should work out exactly how the scene will begin and end and should consider what props they might use (e.g. taking notes during the interviews). All of this teaching needs to take place before the pupils are given the 'making' task in small groups. A class who have made more progress in drama would need less support of this kind.

At one point in the three pigs lesson the participants are given the task of enacting a 'media moment'. They are asked to organise themselves into small groups in order to discuss and re-create a TV broadcast aimed at rebuilding the public image of the wolf (Alex).

> As the groups contemplate positive perspectives of Alex, such as his generosity, his heroism and humanity, the teacher observes how the students are now working against the wolf stereotype. They are required to reconsider a conventional understanding and then decide how their group's interpretation will be communicated within the dramatic artform (*sic*).   (Taylor 2000:16)

This is the crucial point in the lesson that is likely to expose or confirm the group's experience in handling the medium and it is also the point at which some groups will need to be taught how to approach the task. Process drama tends to focus on the significant content and meaning and this is as it should be because not to do so would be to render the whole experience empty. But it is also necessary to recognise the importance of integrating this aspect of the work with the ability to use the medium effectively.

It is significant that it is at the point in both drama projects that small groups are asked to make (in the sense of devise) a piece of drama that the necessity for direct teaching is required. Pupils are able to participate more naturally and spontaneously in such activities as improvised whole-group meetings and 'living through' experiences with teacher in role. They are also able to participate with a minimum of teacher explanation in such activities as questioning in role and still images. The process of devising requires more skill in structuring drama which is one point at which natural participation gives way to a more conscious control of the medium.

One of the significant insights of drama education theorists was to recognise that children are unlikely to create drama of any depth on their own (what is meant by depth will be explored in Chapter 6). But this view derived from an implicit view of drama which was developmental, in which the teacher exploited the pupils' natural propensity for play. It could be argued that one of the ultimate goals of drama teaching should be precisely that pupils should be able to create drama of depth on their own. This may seem to be a betrayal of one of the central beliefs of drama in education practice. However, the question needs to be posed whether there is any logical reason why the experiences which the teacher provides should be qualitatively different from those which pupils create for themselves given an advanced level of development in the subject. A full answer to that question needs a more detailed discussion of 'feeling', also to be undertaken in Chapters 6.

The concept of 'making' is often used as an umbrella term which encompasses various types of work in drama including the process of devising. Bolton, however, uses the term to refer to a 'special category of acting behaviour' in which the participants are 'free to explore without any sense of preparing to show for someone else' (Bolton 1998:274). Within this category he includes the acting behaviours of children's make-believe playing, 'living through' drama and hot-seating. This concept of 'making' has evolved from earlier definitions of drama in education practice: 'type d' or 'drama for understanding' (Bolton 1979, 1984). At no stage did Bolton argue that drama lessons should only include one type of activity but it was clear that the learning in this kind of work was seen to be a 'different order of experience' and was seen as central (1979:11). By 1998 the notion of 'living through' drama has a still important but less emphatic role.

> It represents a hugely important educational and dramatic tool. To ignore 'living through drama', as some recent publications appear to do, is to deprive our pupils of a firm basis for understanding dramatic art. It is not enough to recommend 'improvisation', for much improvisation is mostly performance orientated. The ideal teacher uses the strengths of 'presenting' (including 'performing') *and* 'making'.
> (Bolton 1998:277)

This concept of 'making' and its connection to other forms of drama activity is best understood in relation to progression. Because it has its origins in children's dramatic play it is likely to have a more significant role in primary drama. In fact it is hard to imagine a successful primary drama course without some element of 'living through drama' because the alternatives would be to abandon pupils to their own dramatic playing or to over direct them and risk losing any real sense of engagement. It is no coincidence that the most helpful books on primary drama practice include substantial elements of 'living through' drama. That is not to suggest a simplistic developmental model from 'living through' to 'devising'. With older pupils 'living through' carries more risk but the kind of spontaneity and engagement engendered by a successful experience can provide a foundation for a successful lesson or scheme of work which culminates in performance to an external audience or work on text. It provides a means of balancing structure and experience. To what degree can use of 'living through' be seen as a form of teaching drama? At a simple level it provides pupils with an exemplification of what adopting and sustaining a role involves. More significantly, at its best, it provides an experience of the kind of tension and heightened feeling which is characteristic of the best drama.

Responding

Responding to drama is often conceived in terms of fairly narrow models of theatre. Neelands (1998:ix) has usefully distinguished between the 'literary and private aesthetic tradition of theatre' and the 'oral and communal aesthetic tradition'. The former corresponds more to the popular conception of theatre which involves the performance of plays by professional or amateur actors to a paying audience:

> There is an assumption in this model of theatre that the majority of us will see, rather than be in, such plays. Acting, producing theatre is seen as something only a few can achieve. There is also the assumption that the audience in this literary theatre will be silent and attentive to the work of the actors – audience responses are private rather than publicly shared as they might be in more popular forms of entertainment.
> (ibid:viii)

The 'oral and communal' tradition according to Neelands recognises every member of the group as 'a potential producer – a potential artist'. Theatre is produced 'on the basis of a social agreement between members of a group who come together to make something that will be of importance to them: something that will signify their lives'. The social and community model shares characteristics of drama in schools.

> A school is a community and drama is a living practice within it. The drama that young people make is often based on the concerns, needs and aspirations shared within the school community, or the community of a particular teaching group.
> (Neelands 1998:ix)

This distinction between the two traditions clearly has implications for 'making' drama but there are also consequences for the way in which responding to drama is conceived. A historical and cultural perspective on theatre provides a much wider perspective than the traditional view. Bennett (1997:1) has pointed to the changing relationship between stage and audience worlds through history as well as across cultures and has pointed out that 'conventional notions of theatre and of theatre audiences too often rely on the model of the commercial mainstream'. The development of a passive and elitist audience emerged at a fairly late stage, partly influenced by theatre design:

> After 1850, with the pits replaced by stalls, theatre design ensured the more sedate behaviour of audiences, and the footlights first installed in the

seventeenth-century private playhouses had become a literal barrier which separated the audience and the stage.   (ibid:3)

Bennett (p.19) also points out that Greek, medieval and sixteenth-century audiences functioned in a more active role than is assumed in the traditional model; non-traditional theatre has 'recreated a flexible actor–audience relationship and a participatory spectator/actor'.

Views about the relationship between stage and audience has been informed not just by historical perspectives but also by theoretical insights derived from semiotics and reader response theory. These in turn can illuminate practical approaches in the classroom. Structuralist thinking related to language (from which semiotics was derived) was valuable in moving emphasis away from a view of meaning as something essentially private and derived from personal experience. Instead it drew attention to the importance of relationships between elements of a structure in a public context, a shared system of signification.

> At its simplest, it claims that the nature of every element in any given situation has no significance by itself, and in fact is determined by its relationship to all the other elements involved in that situation. In short, the full significance of any entity or experience cannot be perceived unless and until it is integrated into the *structure* of which it forms a part.   (Hawkes 1991:18)

At a simple level its value in relation to drama is that meaning is not just a function of language but relates to complex and interrelated structures of signs (much school drama in the 1970s and 1980s emphasised language at the expense of other elements). The limitations, however, of structuralist thinking have also been well documented. Its attempts to explain language purely in terms of determinate structures led to accusation of excessive formalism and critics saw a reductive tendency in its narrow focus on binary oppositions (Blake *et al.* 1998:18). Many critics took issue with what they saw as an account of meaning which was closed and mechanically operated. One of Derrida's criticisms was that structuralism failed to account for the 'creative openness' which is an essential feature of language (Lyas 1997:167). There are parallels between structuralist thinking and Wittgenstein's early philosophy in which he sought to give an account of meaning in terms of the logical structure of language. However, his 'picture theory of meaning' went further in emphasising the correspondence between the structure of language and states of affairs in the world. This issue will be discussed in more detail in Chapter 8.

Structuralism as a system of thought has had its advocates as well as its critics. According to Norris (1982:51) it asserts itself where thinking 'yields to the attractions of order and stability'. Its achievements he suggests, quoting Derrida, are intrinsically limited to a reflection of 'the accomplished, the constituted, the constructed' (Derrida 1978:5). What is suppressed is the 'force' or 'animating pressure of intent' which exceeds all the bounds of structure. Human expression redeems signs from the 'fixity of dead convention'. Structuralist thinking 'systematically reduces the human dimension from aesthetic theory' (Sim 1992:431). When content and experience are neutralised in favour of an excessive attention to structure and form it is like 'the architecture of an uninhabited or deserted city, reduced to its skeleton by some catastrophe of nature or art' (Derrida 1978:5).

The words and metaphors in these criticisms group themselves into polarities which echo some of the content of Chapter 2 on structure and experience. On one side we have 'framework, structure, closed, determinate, formalism, mechanism' which are contrasted with concepts like 'openness, creativity, force, animation'. The limitations of structuralism as perceived by poststructuralist thinkers can inform practice in relation to response to drama by reminding us of the need for an 'animating force' to counter the dangers of dealing only in 'dead convention'.

A number of authors have attempted systematic descriptions of the factors which should be taken into account when 'reading' a performance and these have influenced writers on the teaching of drama. Kowzan (quoted in Esslin 1987) identified 13 systems: words, delivery of the text, facial expression, gesture, movement, make-up, hairstyle, costume, props, sets, lighting, music and sound-effects. Esslin in *The Field of Drama* made additions to this list drawing attention to the omission of such elements as the importance of framing and preparatory indicators (the information we are given prior to a performance). He also pointed out that 'all such tables, as all attempts at systematisation of such complex phenomena, must be highly tentative, especially in this field, where the overlap between, and the mutual merging of, the distinct systems, constantly complicates matters' (ibid:105).

Elam (1988) identified broad categories or codes as follows: kinesic (gesture, movement, expression), proxemic (use of space), vestimentary (use of costume), cosmetic (make-up), pictorial (scenes), musical, architectural (stage and playhouse). He also makes clear the overall purpose of his enterprise. We are all he suggests intuitively aware of 'certain potent dramatic and theatrical conventions ruling the structuring and understanding of plays and performances' (ibid:52). He gives examples of being able to distinguish a tragedy from a comedy and 'reading' bits of stylised action and mime on stage. He suggests, however, that 'the precise formulation of the range of rules determining the encoding or decoding of texts is altogether another matter':

> It is the business of semiotics to make these rules explicit, so as to furnish a model of what we might designate the dramatic and theatrical *competence* exercised by experienced performers and spectators.
> (ibid:52)

Other writers who have embarked on a similar quest have included Ubersfeld on the written dramatic text, Dinu on character configuration, Girard, Ouellet and

Rigault, all quoted in Bennett (1997:13). Urian (1998:134) has used the various published schemes to provide a comprehensive spectator's guide to watching plays specifically designed for drama teachers. His intention is to offer 'a framework for spectatorship' which 'aims to give confidence to those teachers uncertain of quite how to approach a theatre visit with their students'. Neelands and Dobson (2000:224) provide a performance analysis questionnaire for use by 17/18 year old students.

Publications like these, particularly the schemes provided by Urian and Neelands and Dobson, are useful particularly because they are aimed primarily at teachers and older students. They are helpful reminders of the wide range of factors which make up the sign system of the theatre. They are also helpful when writing schemes describing progression because they are systematic and 'objective'. The previous discussion of the limitations of structuralism, however, highlights the pitfalls involved if such lists are not employed with caution. Response can be reduced to a systematic, mechanical process devoid of animation and 'force'. There is danger of placing premature emphasis on a cognitive, analytic response and reducing the place and importance of intuition. Such lists do not always distinguish between those factors which might be considered less central (how the production was advertised) and those which are key aspects of a play's meaning. Pupils can spend an inordinate amount of time focusing on the wrong issues or responding in a way which has no authenticity. Helping pupils to respond to performance is not a simple matter of providing them with a systematic framework.

'Responding' then can easily become reduced to a watered-down list of questions adapted from theatre semioticians. 'Response' in the sense of being genuinely engaged and captured by a production can give way to an arid catalogue of atomised observations about lights and acting styles with no 'animation'. There are parallels here with the introduction of the literacy strategy in the United Kingdom which has brought to the whole business of developing language in schools an unprecedented degree of structure. The framework neither guarantees nor necessarily hinders good teaching but it is pontentially dangerous if the life-giving content of 'expression' gives way to the attractions of 'order and stability'. The philosophical misconceptions about language and meaning lurking beneath the surface of the literacy strategy will be explored in Chapter 8.

States, in his account of theatre, criticises an approach which relies purely on a science of signs because it is in danger of missing the essential vitality which a full account of meaning must embrace:

> What is disturbing, if anything, about semiotics is not its narrowness but its almost implicit belief that you have exhausted a thing's interest when you have explained how it works as a sign.   (States 1985:7)

His argument is not that semiotics has no value but that it is only one mode of seeing. It is how the sign system is actually experienced which gives it impact as art. According to States semiotics sees theatre as a process of mediation between artist and culture, theatre and listener: 'theater becomes a passageway for a cargo of meanings being carried back to society after artistic refinement via the language of signs' (ibid:6). His criticism of what he describes as a 'linguistic approach to theatre' is based in part on a referential view of meaning. If we take the view that language does not derive meaning simply by virtue of that to which it refers or in terms of its determinate structures we arrive at a similar conclusion to States but through a different view of language. If we acknowledge that our access to reality is mediated by language then the parallels of art and theatre with language are more telling.

The consequence of these insights is to suggest that meaning in drama is not merely a function of the 'objective', formal qualities of the 'external' sign system. If we relate this to drama teaching, it is not enough for pupils to be able to talk about the scenery, acting and lighting of a play unless this derives from their felt experience of what it means, unless they have been 'grabbed' by it in some way. The intuitive, often raw and immediate reactions of pupils to drama whether in the classroom or theatre should be extended rather than dismissed in favour of more systematic explanations derived from semiotics. This suggests that the starting point should be the work itself rather than a predetermined analytic framework or list of characteristics.

When conceived in terms of traditional practice 'response' is often seen primarily as an analytic/cognitive process and this construct has influenced many of the published schemes. Participants are seen as potential theatre critics passing evaluative opinions and commenting on how meaning is created and conveyed. Pupils who are very strong at making drama often find response of this kind very difficult because they are being asked to rely less on creative, artistic intuition and more on self-conscious analytic skills. Past publications on drama in education tended to make less explicit reference to response than more contemporary publications but that does not mean that response was not implicit in the lessons. Questioning in role (particularly of the actors after a performance), forum theatre, reading the signs of teacher in role can all be interpreted as forms of response. Where devising drama requires an understanding of signs combined to create meaning, forms of 'living through' drama require the ability to read and respond to signs as the drama experience unfolds.

In Chapter 4 it was suggested that two attainment targets might be more helpful than the three which are generally identified by most writers on drama. Although the discussion in this chapter has indicated that in practice 'making' and 'responding' are likely to be integrated to a high degree, the concepts are sufficiently discrete to warrant separate, specific attention when planning and assessing drama. The term 'making' as used here embraced two uses: 'living through' and 'devising'. It has been a central tenet of drama in education theory and practice that 'living through' spontaneous improvisation provides higher 'levels of arousal' than other forms of 'making' (Norman 1999:8). The concept of feeling in drama therefore needs closer discussion.

CHAPTER 6

Working with script: feeling and form

A teacher has asked the class to conduct an improvisation in groups of three. They are to set up a situation which includes a moment of tension. A and B begin the exercise and are then joined by C to create the tension. For example, Adam might be chatting up Becky in a bar; Cathy who is Adam's partner enters and tension ensues. The group are allowed a short time to prepare and then each group shows their work to the rest of the class.

This example comes from Hahlo and Reynolds (2000:21) and is no doubt recognisable as the kind of activity which might occur in a drama workshop. The authors however make the point that this is as it stands a 'flawed exercise'. It is according to them 'too vague' and the participants 'are likely to fall into predictable patterns and traps'. This would be the case for many groups but, from the discussion in the previous chapter, we might want to say that the quality of the exercise needs to be judged in accordance with the experience of the particular group for which it is set. A very experienced group may be able to avoid the pitfalls which the authors identify. They do say that professional actors and school students alike fall into the same trap but of course professional actors may have received training in acting rather than in devising drama.

The basic mistake inexperienced participants make is that they overuse words with a result which is 'generalised, meandering and vague' (ibid:21). The storytelling will be over-elaborate and any attempt at creating tension will be obscured by too much extraneous information:

People will tend to place the exercise in a realistic setting, for instance in an office. There will probably be lots of chat establishing office life, the sort of conversation they think would actually happen across the desks, which will also be littered with signposts designed to give the audience information, such as that they are fed up, working late when most people have gone home. After a while the meat of the scenario might come out, for example: that Adam has got hold of some documents that have been 'borrowed', which Becky is also interested in as they relate to a potentially exciting future project. The required tension arises from the entry of the third character, Cathy, the boss, who is surprised to find them working late and suspects they are up to something. This causes more talk and the elaborate weaving of excuses and half-hearted questioning.

(ibid:22)

The reservations expressed about the way most groups are likely to approach the exercise will be familiar to many drama teachers. The tendency for pupils to think in terms of narrative rather than plot is common (Fleming 1994:53). The work may ramble because it lacks sufficient focus which is an accepted essential element of drama (O'Toole 1992:103). Many teachers will agree with the claim that the attempt to imitate real life causes 'static positioning and overuse of verbal explanation' (Hahlo and Reynolds 2000:22). So far then comments made about this exercise are not unfamiliar. However, the alternative exercise which the authors suggest implicitly raises interesting questions related to the way improvisation and script are sometimes prioritised when teaching drama in schools. A brief summary of the alternative exercise will be given here; the full description can be found in the publication.

Instead of being asked to improvise an extended scenario, the groups are now restricted to five lines of dialogue. They are allowed to plan and rehearse the scene which contains a maximum of five exchanges shared among the three characters. The example given by the authors is as follows:

ADAM: Here are the papers for the new project.
BECKY: Fantastic! How did you get hold of them?
ADAM: This place is like the secret police...
Cathy enters
CATHY: You two are working late...
ADAM: Cathy! We were just thinking of going for a drink.

For the next part of the exercise one of the characters is allowed to make a direct address or 'aside' at any point in the exchange, which provides fresh information. For example Cathy may voice to the audience that the new project has been cancelled. The groups are then asked to add in a theatrical device that contributes to the overall effect, e.g. slow motion, choreographed physical movement, repeated words or phrases. The authors provide some examples of the possibilities:

In our example, Adam and Becky could choreograph their entry into the space from opposite sides with an exaggerated stealth. Cathy could have a long entrance with the sounds of her footsteps echoing, slowed down to increase the dramatic tension. These add in extra layers of dramatic texture that take the scene forward.

(ibid:27)

Again the techniques here are not unfamiliar from the literature on drama teaching; introducing constraint is an established technique. Restricting groups to a specific number of lines is often identified as one approach to writing plays. The use of direct address is also a familiar device. Drama teachers in general are used to the maxim that 'more means less'. What is interesting about this example is the way the types of exercise can be conceived. The first exercise which does not place any constraints on the participants is a form of improvisation. The second activity in which they are confined to five lines could be described as a form of work on script. Some readers might question whether it is accurate to call this a 'script based' exercise which is my description rather than that of the authors. They present this work in their chapter on improvisation rather than in a later chapter which is entitled 'working with text'. Although it is not based on an extract from a play, the exercise uses script in as much as the words spoken are agreed and written down in advance rather than made up on the spot.

It has been implicit in much drama in education practice that the spoken word has primacy over the written, that improvisation has precedence over working with written texts. In *Starting Drama Teaching* I identified a number of reasons why this has been the case:

- the emphasis on creativity and self expression placed more emphasis on spontaneous drama of the pupils' own making rather than working on other people's writing;
- plays tended to be studied in English as literature rather than in the drama classroom;
- the traditional view, challenged by developments in literary theory, assumed that reading was a passive process and that working on text involved simply acting out a script according to the author's intentions;
- practical issues such as the fact that work on scripted drama was more difficult for pupils with limited reading ability than improvisation were also factors.

We could add to this list the view that drama teachers 'often feel that their students are good at improvising scenes and that their confidence and animation disappear when they have to pick up a written text' (Hahlo and Reynolds 2000:141). Somers (1994:80) comments on the neglect of script as follows:

With the widespread adoption of educational drama practice, the scripted play failed to find a regular place in the drama curriculum. This was partly due to the lack of suitable texts but chiefly to the drama movement's belief that it should resist the dominance of the prepared script and encourage the kind of pupil-generated work it saw as central to successful drama teaching.

All of these factors have contributed to the neglect of script but what is missing is an account based on assumptions about language and meaning. It is important to recognise that script is often much more than a record of dialogue but can also include an indication of how setting, character, gestures have been conceived. It is possible to have a script without any dialogue or for stage direction to replace dialogue (e.g. in Beckett's *Acts Without Words*). Nevertheless it can be argued that contrasting assumptions about speech and writing have influenced attitudes to script.

Speech and writing

As suggested in Chapter 5, speech appears on the face of it to be a more natural form of language than writing. We learn to speak before we learn to write. The view advanced by Pinker (1994) that spoken language is an instinct seems to support this view. Thoughts are communicated through speech, and speech exists prior to writing. In speech we can more easily sense the speaker's presence behind the words. It appears more authentic than writing. With speech there is a more obvious link between sound and sense; meaning is yielded more easily and is more transparent.

Writing on the other hand is always conveyed through an extra medium which inhibits the immediacy of the communication. It occupies a public realm where, because it is disembodied from its source, it can be more easily misinterpreted. There is no immediacy, presence or voice that can guarantee its meaning. Writing seems to be a second-hand form of communication that is always removed from its origin. On the basis of these assumptions it is not surprising that improvised drama was given priority over work on script.

Of course the point of dramatising a script is to translate the words on the page into a spoken form, to 'animate' them. However, in the account given here, spontaneous improvisation gives immediate access to more authentic language; why, it might be asked, go through the route of translating script back into spoken language (which after all had its origins with someone else) if the more intimate use of language is available. One obvious answer is based on the cultural heritage justification for drama; teachers work on play texts in order to gain access to drama writing at its best. Let us leave that argument aside for the moment and simply compare pupils' improvised work with their own (or others') written work. This summary of views which gives priority to improvisation over script has been a set of assumptions underlying much drama practice in schools.

However, this 'common sense' picture of language has not gone unchallenged. It may well be that the concept of *writing* gives a much more faithful insight into language and meaning than our intuitive thinking about the spoken word. Because writing is more obviously distant from the consciousness from which it emerged its indeterminacy of meaning is more obvious. The signs we use are never completely under our control; meaning is never static. Language is not transparent, is never simply an 'obedient vehicle of thought' (Norris 1982:30). The transparency which appears in speech is an illusion. For Wittgenstein language has meaning in language games and in 'forms of life', meaning cannot simply be 'present'. Language has meaning not by reference to something outside itself but in cultural contexts. For Derrida meaning is always 'deferred'. Language is always 'inscribed in a network of relays and differential traces' (ibid:29).

If we return to the example of the drama exercise given at the start of this chapter it is clear that certain opportunities occur in the 'script' exercise that were not so readily available in the improvisation. Because of the restrictions placed on the script exercise, the language used becomes more loaded. The meaning is not entirely obvious from the words spoken; clues have to be taken from the context and the non-verbal signals. There is more attention to the language because it is always 'embedded'. There is more opportunity to build in sub-texts because the exchange is so terse. There is more awareness of a lack of transparency in the language. Participants do not mean what they say nor say what they mean.

Hahlo and Reynolds (2000:25) describe their experience of working in this way with a group who worked on a scene about three people sharing a flat:

> Layers of alliance, betrayal and hurt were revealed, as the actors played off each other, and the action was made from moment to moment. The language was heightened and the audience enjoyed the active work of filling in the space around the words.

It is possible to create focus and multi-layers of meaning in a spontaneous improvisation; much of the writing in drama in education in the last 20 years has sought to do just that. The point is not to make crude comparisons which elevates one approach at the expense of the other but to point out the way in which script can paradoxically come closer to 'real' use of language than spontaneous improvisation which appears on the surface to be more 'natural'.

It was acknowledged in the previous chapter that 'living through' drama of which spontaneous improvisation is a primary example has an immediacy and spontaneity which engages pupils (particularly the younger primary age range) in a very absorbing way. However, spontaneous improvisation is much more difficult to sustain than has been acknowledged in much of the history of drama teaching. Young children engaged in dramatic play do use language in what appears to be a free and unconscious way. However, pupils often find improvised drama very challenging; they can feel very exposed and often do not know what to say. They may obligingly attempt to keep things going but can easily change the focus of the scene in unhelpful ways. There may be a tendency to want to lay the necessary information out in excessive detail, to build in a background history for each character. It is often too much in a spontaneous improvisation to expect subtlety, nuance, density of meaning, hints, ambiguities, 'footprints' and 'traces' of meaning; it is hard enough keeping the words flowing. Spontaneous improvisation can sometimes feel like a dinner party which has fallen a bit flat which the participants are bravely trying to resuscitate.

This is not an argument for abandoning improvisation in favour of script but there is a case for suggesting that script should occupy a more prominent place than has been the norm in much drama teaching, particularly with older pupils. One case for spontaneous improvisation is that the speech is more natural. However, language is more appropriately seen as pertaining to culture than to nature and one of the values of engagement in dramatic activity is to draw attention to the way meaning derives from context and not in relation to the thought and intentions of the speaker. Chapter 8 will discuss the degree to which language in drama (of whatever form) is less 'natural' than the language of everyday conversation.

This discussion began with a consideration of the various reasons why work on text has been neglected in the drama in education tradition. We could add to that list the importance of feeling, summed up by Norman (1999:12). One of the vital elements of drama is described as follows:

> Experiencing the 'here and now' of the drama with high levels of feeling engagement and motivation, both in and out of and about the drama. For me this would always involve some element of whole group work and Teacher in Role.

The assumption here that 'feeling engagement' only happens through a certain type of practice in order to provide 'high levels of arousal' was a central tenet of much drama in education theory and practice. The issue was addressed in the previous chapter in the discussion of 'making' in relation to 'devising' and 'living through' forms of drama where it was suggested that a closer examination of 'feeling' in drama is needed.

Feeling and form

Feeling has lost some of its prominence in writing about the teaching of drama. To some degree this reflects wider changes in educational discourse. In England the dominant preoccupation is with targets, outcomes, frameworks and measurement. The obsession with efficiency and 'means' referred to in Chapter 1 has changed priorities. It is difficult to take account of feelings when assessing drama or describing the way pupils make progress in the subject. Broadfoot (2000:214) refers to the 'ennui' which has infected education. 'The magic and mystery of emotion which can bring the whole process alive is subsumed to the necessity of covering the syllabus and doing what is required for the exam.' As well as being influenced by the prevailing *zeitgeist*, there may be other, more theoretical reasons for the reduction in references to emotion and feeling in writing about drama. Slade and Way have become fairly easy targets to chastise for having espoused ideas about creativity and self expression in the 1950s and 1960s. Authors who write with too much enthusiasm about expressing feelings in drama run the risk of being accused of subjectivism, dualism or sentimental romanticism.

This is a curious state of affairs. Drama is an art form. Art is to most people intuitively about expression and certainly about feeling and emotions. To understand the theoretical backlash against reference to emotions and feelings it will be helpful to consider briefly the way ideas on these concepts have developed in aesthetic theory. In common with many writers I will not distinguish between the terms 'feeling' and 'emotion' in the discussion which follows.

Tolstoy is the writer most closely associate with self expression in art. He expressed his views as follows:

> To evoke in oneself a feeling one has once experienced, and having evoked it in oneself, then, by means of movements, lines, colours, sounds, or forms expressed in words, so to transmit that feeling that others may experience the same feeling – this is the activity of art. Art is a human activity consisting in this, that one man consciously by means of certain external signs, hands onto others feelings he has lived through, and that others are infected by those feelings and also experience them.   (Tolstoy 1996:51)

There are now some well known arguments against self expression in aesthetics (Hospers 1969, Tormey 1971) and several summaries are available (Wilkinson 1992:179, Lyas 1997:59, Fleming 1994:163). One aspect of the theory is the assumption that artists have *particular* feelings when creating works of art. The counter argument is simply that what we learn from artists themselves contradicts that claim. Artists might just as easily be motivated by feelings associated with the desire to make money or they may simply have been concentrating on getting their technique right. As Eaton (1988:25) says, 'Many (artists) specifically deny that they felt happy when they wrote their happiest work.' To claim that artists have particular feelings during creation also seems 'inconsistent with what we know about their lives at a particular time'. She goes on to quote the unofficial self-portrait by Rembrandt which was painted at a time when his life was full of sorrow but actually depicts the artist laughing.

Another problem with the theory concerns the relation between the art work and the audience or spectator, which is sometimes referred to as the 'reception problem' (Hughes 1993). If the purpose of the work is to arouse the same feelings which were experienced by the artist it suggests that all those viewing the work will have the same response (which again does not accord with actual experience). A useful parallel can be made between the self expression theory of art and the view of language and meaning which has been addressed at various times in this book. Hospers (1969:166) includes Tolstoy's theory under the heading 'art as emotional communication'. The theory of self expression assumes that the work of art is 'transparent' in that 'it acts as a window through which the viewer registers, and sympathetically responds to, the feelings of the artist' (Hughes 1993:39). A naive theory of language and communication assumes likewise that language is transparent, that it acts as a simple conduit between the thoughts in the speaker's head and those evoked in the listener. Instead we need to think of meaning in relation to use in public contexts (in the case of language) and feeling in relation to the art product (in the case of art).

In the case of the Rembrandt painting we can say that it embodies or expresses happiness without claiming that the artist *necessarily* experienced such emotions when creating or viewing the work or the spectator *necessarily* experiences such emotions when viewing it. It may happen to make people feel happy when they see it but that is not the key aesthetic explanation of feeling in relation to the work. In the case of drama the situation becomes more complex because the art 'product' consists of human beings (actors or participants in a workshop) who themselves have particular feelings. For that reason it has often been argued that in a drama the way the participants actually feel is a key defining characteristic of its quality.

Lyas (1997:63) makes a distinction between what may be expresssed by the characters *in* a work and what may be expressed *by* a work in its portrayal of those characters.

> Camus's *The plague* contains a number of characters who express certain views, but, in addition, the novel itself articulates an attitude. Rembrandt's astonishing Girl Sleeping shows us a girl asleep, but the picture itself expresses a tenderness towards the sleeper.

On the basis of this distinction it makes sense to say that a particular drama expresses or embodies a certain feeling without claiming that the participants must be feeling in a particular way. In the case of the exercise described at the start of this chapter the scripted exchange might evoke tension and feelings of rivalry and jealousy. However, it is not necessary to claim that the participants actually experience those feelings. It is also possible (on the basis of the distinction made by Lyas) to say that the participants (as authors of the piece) are in some sense 'expressing feelings' in that they are embodying feelings in the form discussed further in Chapter 9.

Hughes (1993) has drawn attention to the conceptual links between Tolstoy's theory of art and Stanislavski's analysis of the art of acting. Tolstoy's *What is Art?* was published in 1896 and Stanislavski founded the Moscow Art Theatre eight years later. What Hughes calls a Tolstoyean theory of acting suggests that 'the task of the actor is to engender emotions in the audience by evoking them in himself' (p.40). Stanislavsky's methods changed from use of 'affective memory' (the actor evokes the feeling by searching for a parallel moment in his own life) towards a system of 'physical action' (the actor works to find the emotion through the physical actions) but Hughes suggests that like Tolstoy, he relied on an 'oversimplified model of the interaction between actors and audience. The result was that he never allowed the play to speak for itself' (p.46).

On the basis of this view it is easier to see the relationship between feeling and form. If we say that pupils are 'expressing feelings' in a drama this only becomes problematic if we assume some kind of temporal distinction between 'having the feeling' and 'expresssing it' or if we assume that the way pupils feel is related to the drama in a *specific* way. The discussion in Chapter 1 used practical examples to illustrate the dynamic relationship between form and content. In both cases the meaning related to the thematic content emerged in a social context from inside the construction of the drama. The creative process emphasised the making of the drama and did not seek to highlight significant meaning in advance. The learning and understanding emerged through expression. Similarly the significant feeling was evoked by the work and attached to the form rather than to the participants.

Drama in education writers have explained the importance of feeling and emotion in relation to drama in different ways. At one stage it was assumed that an individual participant in drama should experience 'real' feelings; this was what 'depth' in drama meant: a criterion of good work was the extent to which the participants in an improvisation 'suffered the relevant emotions'. An explanation of this history is found in Bolton (1998:220). It was also recognised, however, that a group might share the same feelings in a drama, 'the participants collectively suffer fear, anxiety, sadness, disappointment, hope or relief' (ibid:200). A third explanation was to see the feeling content of the drama as belonging to the participants as percipients or spectators (Fleming 1985:9). In other words, in an improvised drama about an escape from prison which contains a 'moment of awe' we might want to say (a) that the pupils are experiencing individual emotions of guilt, relief, anger or (b) they are all experiencing a feeling of betrayal or (c) they are experiencing feelings as an audience would when looking at the work. All of these explanations, however, are looking in the wrong direction, trying to locate the feeling in the pupils, rather than in the form.

That does not mean that pupils' feelings are not important in drama. We want pupils to feel engaged, interested, committed, enthusiastic, tense, excited. We do not want them to feel bored or uninterested. However, to try to make them feel a particular emotion in relation to the drama or to try to judge the drama in relation to their feelings is to miss the point. In *Starting Drama Teaching* I mistakenly held on to a notion of 'feeling response' in judging the quality of the drama. I am aware that challenging this view seems to be a betrayal of a central tenet of drama in education. It has always been a central belief that pupils should have authentic feelings and not be asked to switch on emotional display. Bolton (1998:200) describes this process as follows, 'they resort to pretending feelings as though they were in a traditional drama where characters are required to show their feeling of "surprise" or "hate" or jealousy or amusement to an audience'. However, the appropriate explanation in these cases is to say that the pupils have not been helped to use the dramatic form appropriately. They have been taught to act badly. How, for example, do we judge that they are 'pretending', except by judging that the drama itself (i.e. their attempts to show emotion) is not embodying feeling in any successful way?

Drama in education has tended to associate the concept of 'depth' with 'feeling'. On the basis of this discussion however it makes more sense to explain depth primarily in terms of the content and form. One of the ways in which depth is created in a drama is by multi-layers of meaning through the form of the work. This is one way of making the content 'significant', a term introduced in Chapter 1. A tableau or exchange of dialogue may remain one dimensional and banal unless its authors seek to inject a meaning below the surface appearance. Dramatic irony always adds depth because an extra level of interpretation is introduced. The meaning of dialogue can be given more depth and poignancy by the use of framing actions which precede it and change its meaning (Fleming 1997b). None of this is to deny that emotions and feelings are an important part of the drama and that pupils as actors and spectators *may* experience strong feelings in the course of the work (just as they may do so when reading about the death of Lennie in *Of Mice and Men* or when writing their own sad story). The teacher's aim, however, is not to arouse feelings but to help the pupils to create work which embodies them.

On the basis of the discussion so far in this chapter there is no logical or theoretical reason why feeling should be more significant in relation to work based on improvised drama than it is on work with script. It often seems that way because working with script seems more artificial and awkward. However, it is a practical, pedagogical distinction rather than a theoretical and conceptual one. Improvised drama is likely to feel more immediate and intense, it is often easier for participants to feel more engaged but that makes it an extremely useful technique in the repertoire of drama teachers rather than a way of evoking a particular kind of unique feeling in relation to the content of the drama. In fact if the definition of 'script' is widened the affinity between script and improvisation becomes clearer.

When categorising drama activities and trying to show different family resemblances it seems on the surface that 'spontaneous improvisation' and 'planned improvisation' have more in common than work on script. The language used certainly suggests that this is the case. However, if a planned improvisation (which is almost a contradiction in terms) is short enough for the dialogue and actions to be memorised then this amounts to a 'script' even though nothing may be written down. On the other hand, if the planned improvisation is not short enough to be memorised then the work often starts to resemble a spontaneous improvisation. This often happens when pupils are presenting work which they have planned in advance which turns out to be different each time. Even a spontaneous improvisation may need to 'script' the setting, characters and context even though the words are not preplanned.

The point being made here is different from the one Bolton makes when he suggests that a teacher in role is providing a 'script' or 'text' to be read by the pupils, that this is a script 'in the making', although that is also of course a legitimate use of the term (1998:183). It is possible to write a script to capture a drama after it has finished. I am, however, using script to refer to those elements on which the drama is based, even though these may not be literally written down. There are parallels here with Derrida's concept of 'writing' which he uses to draw attention to characteristics of language which exist 'prior to any "inscription" in the ordinary sense – with ink on paper' (Staten 1986:61). The point of this discussion is not just a semantic one which revolves around a definition of script. The point is to ease the transition from one form of activity in drama to another (an approach which is invited by the theoretical discussion).

Kempe and Ashwell (2000:215) refer to 'desk-bound' and 'stage-bound' models of teaching dramatic literature. In the first case the pupils are confined to reading the play around the class, answering comprehension questions and writing critical essays. The only alternative practical approach was often thought to be working towards an actual production which is often difficult for practical reasons but also the learning outcomes are often 'highly differentiated'.

> For example a student playing Lady Macbeth may understandably be so concerned to get her bit 'right' that innumerable other points of interest are simply blocked out . . . as the first night approaches, opportunities for learning about the play, through reflective discussion tend to dissolve in the furious rush to iron out a myriad of practical problems.

They go on to say that pupils can learn a great deal about the way scripts work by 'reading, writing and playing around with very short pieces of dialogue' (ibid:216). It is important to acknowledge that speaking words that have been written by someone else can feel awkward; there is always the potential for having problems with actual reading and stumbling over pronunciation. But these are largely pedagogical challenges. The key issue is for the participants to have a sense of ownership of the language which in practical terms often will mean an approach through workshops, mixing work on text with other drama activities.

Learning by heart has gone out a fashion in education because it has for a long time been associated with mindless drilling and authoritarianism. Blake *et al.* (1998:145) make the point that rote learning is often connected with a distinction between deep and surface learning.

> Surface learning treats everything as not relatable or anchorable, concentrating on memorising bits of information. Deep learning aims at understanding meaning by relating it to established ideas. There are facts and there are thinking skills. Facts become meaningful when thinking locates them in

cognitive structures. What is to be learned may be anchorable in cognitive structures or it may consist in relatively isolated bits of information.

They go on, however, to suggest that the metaphor of surface and depth may reflect an 'essentialism' that is blind to the way signs actually function. A traditional argument against learning by heart is that it is possible that we may be forced to learn words we do not fully understand. But what sense do we make of 'fully understand' in this case? Understanding is not an all or nothing affair. Surface learning may be but a first and necessary step on a route to a deeper learning. If something is learned by heart, it becomes familiar.

> Familiarity, a kind of habituation, is evident in various aspects of learning . . . the fact that the words that we have learned makes (these) particular thoughts possible . . . . Something seems to have been laid in store, something whose future was unclear.
> (ibid:146)

An obsession with 'complete' understanding which contains a misguided view of the way language has meaning may prevent us from absorbing language whose meaning we do not fully grasp but whose resonance may haunt us and continue to unfold. Many of the practical approaches to Shakespeare verse developed in recent years do not seek to uncover meaning in advance of use and enjoying the text.

> What I want you to feel from these exercises is this: because you are becoming familiar with the language in ways that are not to do with thinking harder, but to do with receiving it in more instinctive ways, you will then not press the meaning out through stress, and words will then have much more life and colour.
> (Berry 1993:170)

This is not to argue that pupils should be drilled into learning lines by heart in an authoritarian fashion. It does however suggest that memorising lines either through workshop activities or for a production has more educational potential than has often been assumed.

Approaches to script

The practical implications of the above discussion is to suggest that although working with script (either the pupils' own writing or published play texts) is often a pedagogical challenge, its place in the drama classroom should be unquestioned, particularly with older pupils. It is precisely the pedagogic techniques associated with drama in education which can be used to make script more accessible. Winston (2000:75) provides a detailed example of a project on *Macbeth* with a Year 6 (10 year olds) which integrates work on the script with a conventions approach to the drama. In the course of four lessons the project includes teacher in role (as Duncan providing a monologue which gives details of the battle), still images (to represent the qualities of Macbeth as understood so far), games (blindman's bluff used to taunt Macbeth), conscience alley (articulating reasons for and against killing the king), hot-seat (to question Macbeth on suspicion of committing the murder). At the same time the children include direct work on the text in the course of the lessons, e.g. they use the text of the play to evoke atmosphere (using lines from the opening witches scene), to greet Macbeth ('All hail Macbeth, hail to thee Thane of Glamis') and to perform an extract from Act 4, scene 1 (in which the witches give their prophecy).

Woolland (1993:170) has commented that there is 'an understandable wariness about using scripts in primary schools because it is sometimes feared that they can intimidate children and inhibit the children's own creative work'. He goes on, however, to point out that script can be used in a creative rather than restrictive way with young pupils. For example a script does not have to take a conventional form but may be reproduced as a storyboard, a comic strip or a simple summary of scenes.

Practical approaches to working with script can be found in a number of publications (Kempe and Ashwell 2000, Hahlo and Reynolds 2000, Bennathan 2000, Kempe and Warner 1997, Fleming 1997b). The sample of activities given below have been summarised to illustrate the way in which drama work on script treats language seriously. The intention, however, is not to overemphasise the importance of language; several of the activities draw attention to the way non-verbal signs affect meaning. But that too is to treat language seriously, to recognise its limitations as well as its possibilities.

Examples

Creating the sub-text

Examples of this exercise can be found in a number of publications (Fleming 1994:108, Kempe and Ashwell 2000:221). The idea here is for the participants to supply the thoughts of the characters in an exchange of dialogue. The sub-text can either refer to the intended meaning which is conveyed by tone and gesture or the concealed thoughts which are not articulated. Thus if a character says, 'Would you like to pop in for a cup of tea?', the words may run counter to the actual meaning conveyed ('I am only asking this out of politeness and do not expect you to say yes'). Alternatively the thoughts may be different from the spoken words. 'Please say no.' It could be argued that the second case is not strictly speaking an example of sub-text but it is well to be aware of the ways in which participants may interpret the activity. The script can be drawn from a play text or written by the participants themselves. This exercise on sub-text highlights the way in which meaning is not 'present' simply in the words spoken but is a function of the context and non-verbal signs. It can also show how meaning is not simply a function of intention. Do we, for example, attribute the meaning of the utterance to the way it is understood or to the thoughts of the speaker?

Enacting the sub-text

This activity can be combined with the preceding one. Here the sub-text is already supplied (either in advance by the teacher or by having groups swop their scripts) and the idea is that the participants try to convey the sub-text without actually articulating it aloud, using only the script. Inititially participants may only think of using tone of voice but they can be encouraged to think about the way physical proximity, actions, gesture, pace of delivery can all change what is conveyed by the same words. A simple exchange can seem to convey entirely different meanings: I love you; I hate you; I am bored by you; I am intimidated by you.

Communicating the sub-text

The emphasis is slightly different from the previous activity. Two people are given the script of a dialogue. One of them is given separate information about the 'message' to the other underlying the surface meaning of the words and the other has to react accordingly. This approach is using a technique fairly common in drama in education practice whereby tension is created by providing one of the pair with information which is withheld from the other. For example, when making final plans for a holiday, one of the friends wants to back out.

Contrasting ways of recording narrative and plot

Pupils are given examples of the same narrative in different formats (cartoon with speech bubbles, prose narrative, play script). They are asked how information is presented differently in each case. This is a useful way of introducing conventions of script to younger pupils and is getting them to think about drama as a genre (Barlow and Skidmore 1994:92).

Experiment with words or pairs of words

The class are asked to say 'good bye' in as many different ways as they can: scared, happy, angry, worried (Barlow and Skidmore 1994:93). They are then invited to create a dialogue between two people consisting of the words 'you' and 'me'. Each participant can use either word as many times as they want. The exercise can be extended by including 'yes' and 'no' (Hahlo and Reynolds 2000:142). This exercise encourages participants to listen and try to pick up possible meanings from tone and non-verbal clues. Alternatively a group may be given an expression such as 'Mmmmmmm!' and try to convey different meanings such as a suppressed scream, a murmour of admiration or dissent (Somers 1994:87).

Use exaggerated physical actions

Pairs are given an extract from a play which has a fair amount of implied or explicit physical action. They are asked to write down actions to go with each sentence or even phrase. The actors then experiment with the actions using them in different combinations: saying and doing the action as well as saying the text; doing the action and saying the text; say the text without saying the action or physically doing it. The idea is that the exaggerated physical action will leave a trace element on the original language and it will be brought alive. A detailed example of this activity is given by Hahlo and Reynolds (2000:168) using an example from *The Cherry Orchard*. Gibson (1998:176) provides an example of the way actions can illuminate the meaning of a Shakespeare extract.

Working with stage directions

The teacher gives the class an extract from a play without including the stage extracts. They discuss briefly what they make of it. They are then given the extract which now includes the stage directions and try it out before they attempt to write their own short script (Kempe and Ashwell 2000:218). Another approach might be to attempt to categorise the different functions served by stage directions: in relation to the scene: stage lay-out, props; in relation to the actors: tone, actions, emotion, movement (Wallis and Shepherd 1998:9).

Identifying implicit stage directions

Shakespeare's plays largely embedded the actions in the dialogue. Full stage directions only developed in the nineteenth century but as Wallis and Shepherd (1998) have pointed out many directions in modern texts are still implicit in the words spoken. Asking pupils to identify stage directions in the dialogue is a reminder that the meaning does not just reside in the language spoken and that plays were written for performance. Older pupils can be asked to look at different approaches to stage directions in, for example, plays by Shaw, Miller and Bond.

Acting out dialogue in different ways

Groups are given a short sequence of simple dialogue and try out different ways of acting it out (Fleming 1994:108). They do not change the actual words but can change the tone, pace and actions which accompany the words. Kempe and Ashwell (2000:216) extend this exercise by including an element of response (other pupils have to comment on how successful the group has been in making the context clear) and further script writing (groups write their own short script and pass it on to another group to interpret).

Using sounds and noises

In *Equus* Act 1, scenes 20 and 21 Shaffer uses the chorus of the 'Equus noise' to accompany the riding of the Equus at night. Jones (in Nicholson 2000:122) describes how she asked pupils to create the noise using a range of vocal sounds. She links this work to Artaud's challenge to a narrow concept of 'dialogue theatre' (in which language is too dominant). When working with script it is important to guard against reducing physicality (a tendency pupils can easily fall into) and to reduce the sensuousness of language (another form of 'essentialism').

Creating a context
The pupils are given a short section of dialogue from a play (or lines written by the teacher) from which the contextual details (place, setting, names of characters) have been deleted. Their task is to create a context and try out the scene (Somers 1994:88).

Creating irony
Pupils are given four lines of dialogue and asked to invent two contexts, one of which is straightforward, the other contains some element of irony which is injected not by changing the words but by changing the situation (Fleming 1997b:85). A simple line such as 'This drink tastes good' becomes much more highly charged if the speaker is in the process of being poisoned.

Linking text
Pupils are given different lines from a play. Their task is to move around the room saying the lines and trying to find out who else in the group has lines spoken by the same character (Kempe and Warner 1997:vii).

Writing scripts
Writing a script for a play not only provides an insight into the way drama works but also provides tacit illumination of language and meaning (in a way that is different from poetry and the novel). Drama's primary language mode is dialogue and it is more evident that meaning is created 'between' rather than 'within' people. The following list of questions (adapted from Fleming 2001) can be addressed with pupils in relation to the writing of scripts.

- What type of audience 'framing' is required for the play? What information needs to be given before the opening and what form should that take (title, introductory information, set, action on stage before opening lines)? Plays from different times, e.g. Miller's *The Crucible* and Shakespeare's *Julius Caesar* could be used to demonstrate very different approaches.
- How will necessary information be given to the audience? Will this be contained in the dialogue or is there a danger that this will appear false and artificial? The beginning of Stoppard's *The Real Inspector Hound* parodies badly handled exposition in an amusing way.

- Does the written script need to specify a particular setting or set design? Should this be included in the stage directions or should it be left to interpretation? Is a particular size and type of space implied? Why, for example, is such a minimal set required for *Waiting for Godot?*
- Should the required actions and expressions be stated explicitly or is it enough for these to be implied in the dialogue? For example, if a word like 'angrily' is not included in brackets in the text does this leave too much license for interpretation by actors and director?
- How is information conveyed differently in written dialogue from narrative? What challenges does this bring for the playwright? How do playwrights give us access to people's motivation, intention and thoughts? We need to see Iago plotting before the scene in which he tricks *Othello*, otherwise we would not understand his motive; a novelist can achieve this through prose description.
- What structural aspects need to be taken into account when writing plays? Examples include: division into scenes; constructing a dramatic plot from a narrative; experimenting with time (flashbacks, non-linear narratives), devices for creating dramatic tension, dramatic irony.
- What dramatic techniques which pupils may have used in their improvised drama can be used in scripted work? Examples of these include direct address to the audience, asides, moving in and out of role, use of chorus, expressing inner thoughts.
- How does the language of drama differ from everyday speech? Pupils often assume that a dramatic script is simply recorded conversation but in fact it generally has less redundancy, is more ordered and tends to carry more information.

These activities provide examples of ways of working with script. The intention is not to suggest that work on script should only be undertaken in relation to very short extracts. Exercises of this kind can be combined to approach the active study of an entire play. Of course another approach is for the group to turn the play into a performance, a concept which will discussed in the next chapter.

CHAPTER 7

Performing drama: process and product

At a signal from the teacher each group presents the drama which they have been working on for most of the lesson. The first group begins with a fairly ordinary breakfast scene. It starts slowly with just one character 'on stage' who sets the scene with one or two simple actions. As the other family members enter they exchange dialogue which is at first fairly terse and slow, but gradually gathers pace and volume. The scene has all the potential for cliché but the dialogue is given extra depth by the efforts of one of the teenage sons to make his voice heard amidst the chatter. He is not being ignored completely but he is not being properly listened to. It is clear from the snatches of dialogue that his exams are coming up and that he is a high achiever. The scene changes and the family are now gathered around a bed in a hospital. From off-stage a voice can be heard as if of a policeman asking questions of different members of the family. It becomes apparent that the son has taken an overdose. The pieces presented by each group have a common theme: the inability of someone to make his or her voice heard (child abuse victim, businessman, teacher). At the end of the final presentation one of the pupils reads aloud Stevie Smith's poem *Not Waving But Drowning*.

Elsewhere in a primary school the class are about to present their play based on the Irish Potato Famine. It consists of a number of different scenes which together give an account of the discovery and spread of the blight. Each scene is linked to the next by one of the pupils whose narrative gives an overview of the historical facts. All the pupils are involved although their relative contributions vary. In one scene a woman with a bundle of clothes in her arms to represent a baby is seen calling at different houses and stopping people in the street to beg for money. When she arrives back at her own house she conceals the truth of what she has been doing from the rest of her family.

In a different school several groups of pupils have presented their drama and now it is the turn of the last group to take their turn. It is clear from their introductory exposition that a man is at home alone with his young son. A knock comes to the door and two social workers arrive. They have a court order to take the young child into care. The scene becomes chaotic and noisy as the child resists and physical force has to be used. The disruption finally gives way to calm as the man is left alone in the house with his face set motionless. In his hands he holds a music box which his child has given him before he leaves which he sets playing.

Is it accurate to describe each of these presentations (as they have been described here) as a performance? Our every day use of the term suggests that it would. The pupils are communicating meaning to an audience (the rest of class) which seems to fulfil the necessary criteria. However, many writers in the past, as well as more recent approaches in the history of drama in education, have sought to preserve a distinction between 'performance' and other forms of communication activity in drama such as 'presenting', 'sharing', 'showing'. To throw some light on the use of terms it will be helpful to look in some detail at the context in which each piece of work took place.

Not Waving But Drowning

A version of this project which is presented here in summary form is described in more detail in *The Secondary English Magazine* (Fleming 1999a). It was taught with a class of 14 year old pupils who were fairly experienced in devising small group drama.

1. The pupils gather in a circle and play a simple warm up game creating in pairs still images in the centre of the circle. The images which the pupils form are both realistic (two people waiting at a bus-stop, one photographing the other) and abstract. The nature of the warm up is not that important but this one provides a useful lead-in to tableau which follows.

2. In small groups pupils depict a situation involving bullying of some kind. They then recreate the tableau injecting more depth and meaning (by articulating the thoughts of the characters involved, by creating another tableau in which the bully in one is the victim in another, by reading an extract from the victim's diary to accompany the tableau). The teacher then role plays a situation with one of the pupils in which the bullying victim tries unsuccessfully to tell someone in authority about what has happened (they may be unable to convey the facts or may be able to convey the facts but not the seriousness of the effect).

3. In the same groups pupils enact a situation in which one person tries to confide a problem to an older person (pupil/teacher, worker/boss, child/parent) but is not successful either because they are unable to disclose the problem or because the other person is too preoccupied. This is juxtaposed against a different brief scene in which the nature of the problem is revealed. This activity introduces the notion of 'juxtaposition' in a very tightly structured way so that the participants can learn the technique. Scene one might show the pupil unable to get a word in with the teacher who is demanding

homework; the second scene could then show the pupil at home being given excessive and unreasonable responsibility for younger siblings.

4. The main part of the workshop now takes place. The groups are given the following two lines of text and are asked to brainstorm possible contexts to which the words might apply. The groups report back on the result of the brainstorm.

> They thought he was doing fine.
> How very seriously wrong they were.

Typical suggestions for contexts might be as follows: a pupil being bullied at school (staying with the earlier theme); a teacher in a new, challenging job; a businessman in financial trouble; a recovering alcoholic; a child suffering abuse at home. Some groups may pick up on the serious tone of the second line especially with the inclusion of the word 'very', others may not and may create more light-hearted situations.

5. They are now asked to create two pieces of drama based on the quotation, one showing why 'they' thought he was 'doing fine'; the other showing the reality. Both scenes will be presented to the rest of the class. The responsibility for the work is now handed over to the class. The groups do not have to confine themselves to naturalistic enactment – they might use tableau, inner thoughts, monologues or other conventions. They may need to be advised specifically not to try to present a complicated plot and may be helped if the teacher provides an example drawn from one of the contexts suggested in the brainstorm: the first scene might show a family gathering in which the busy activity and banter leaves no space for the teenage daughter to voice her worries; the second scene takes the form either of a conversation with a close friend or a monologue in the form of a diary which reveals her real anxieties about bullying at school. Alternatively a company director at a business meeting conceals the truth of his financial desperation which is revealed in the next scene during a telephone conversation with the bank.

6. Copies of the poem Stevie Smith's *Not Waving But Drowning* are distributed and it is read aloud by the teacher. The pupils are asked to think about the literal content (a man drowns because of an unfortunate misunderstanding) and then to consider the metaphorical meaning by relating the poem to the scenarios they have created. The work of each group is now performed and juxtaposed with a reading of the poem.

The Potato Famine

This project was taught with a Year 5 class (ten year olds). A more detailed adapted version of the work can be found in *Drama 9–11* (Chaplin 1999) which also contains the picture and facsimiles of the documents used.

The topic was introduced by showing the class a picture of a family gathered outside their thatched cottage clearly upset about something. The pupils are asked to say what they can deduce from the picture, e.g. it is some time in the past; it is in the country; the people seem quite poor; it seems to be some kind of farm; it may be one large family; the house is small for one family; they seem to be quite sad; they are gathered together for some reason. The class are asked to speculate on the type of life these people lived. What means of transport might they have had? Did they have electricity, telephones, television? What means of entertainment did they have? At this point the pupils are informed that the scene is set in Ireland and they are asked whether that piece of information provided any more clues. Would the people have spoken differently? How long ago might this be?

The pupils are invited to find out more about the situation by asking questions of one or more of the people in the picture (teacher in role). Certain aspects of the context are invented (e.g. the nature of the family relationships) but the teacher in role is used to convey background information: all the potatoes are rotten; nobody knows why the potatoes have gone bad; the house and small piece of land are rented not owned; the landlord or his agent have to be paid rent; the potato is the main source of food – that is why the situation is so serious; a small number of other crops are grown but these have to be used for rent; the family live a very simple but happy life; the potatoes are also used to feed the small number of animals.

The pupils act out a short scene in which one member of the family goes to a neighbour to see if they have any food to spare, only to find that their potatoes are rotten as well. Because the structure and outcome of this scene is predetermined, the pupils can concentrate their energies on devising the drama. The aim is to use dramatic form to simulate the spread of the bad news of the crop failure and to increase pupils' understanding of the circumstances and context of the events. A series of questions and suggestions helps the pupils construct their scene. What is the neighbour doing when the visitor arrives? The visitor does not want to come straight to the point and ask outright for food – what does he/she talk about first? The neighbour has not started harvesting yet and the two of them go to dig up some potatoes – what sort of mime would be appropriate? The two neighbours wonder what the causes of the crop failure are – what reasons do they give? How worried would the neighbours be at this stage? An 'eavesdropping' or 'open door' technique gives pupils experience of sharing their drama without placing too much pressure on them to 'perform' at this stage.

By combining pairs into fours and fours into eights the pupils simulate the spread of gossip. This is an appropriate point to introduce more detailed information about the crop failure to be incorporated into the scenes. What would a potato plant have looked like? From what part of the plant did the potatoes come? The disease appeared at first as dark spots on the leaves, followed by a furry growth. The stem and leaves started to decay. The tubers turned black and went into a pulp which smelled very bad. At first the people tried to save the sound parts of the tubers but soon the entire crop was rotten. All sorts of reasons were given for the crop failure: use of the wrong type of manure, frost, the thunderstorms and rain, an act of God, even if the potatoes looked sound when dug up they would turn black in a few days.

The pupils confront the landlord (teacher in role) about the high rents and the lack of food. This is conducted as 'living through' spontaneous improvisation. This is a more 'expressive' than 'representational' piece of work. Inevitably it strays from the historical accuracy (at one point the pupils became attached to the idea that the landlord was poisoning the potatoes) but it enhances their engagement with the content and provides an opportunity for them (as pupils as much as peasants) to express their indignation about the injustice.

The pupils prepare a scene which included the following dimension: one member of the family resorts to begging but is too ashamed to admit this to the others. The aim of this activity was to give pupils some insight into how people may have wished to retain their dignity and self-respect despite the hardship. They discuss why people resorted to begging and what they might have felt about having to do so. The pupils are given specific help with the following aspects of their drama: choosing a scene (e.g. mealtime when for the first time the family have something substantial to eat; bedtime and mother has not yet returned home); deciding on a beginning (e.g one of the parents is trying to play a game with the children to distract them from their hunger) including appropriate actions (e.g. how might the family be affected by their hunger?); deciding on an effective ending (e.g. what makes the family suspicious? how do they react when they discover the truth?).

Other activities included in the project were as follows: group tableau showing an eviction (they compared their version to a picture of the time showing the same scene); hot-seating of people who were witnesses to the closing of one of the soup kitchens (before this activity they read historical documents from the time announcing the closure); writing of short scripts of the conversations which took place when one or two of the family members were forced to go to the workhouse (they are given information about the conditions and advice on setting out the script); voicing of the thoughts of one of the family members as he is about to emigrate, expressing his conflicting feelings.

It was only after a considerable amount of process work, contextualisation and 'scene setting' that the pupils 'performed' their work, not to an external audience but to each other. The intention was for the pupils to intersperse a narrative text with various dramatic presentations to form a unified product. This activity consolidated their previous work. The presentations took the form of polished improvisations, mimes, scripted exchanges and tableaux. The addition of music faded in and out between scenes enhanced the final product.

Charlie Foster

The third presentation described at the start of this chapter derived from a project which used teacher in role as a stimulus for the pupils' own devising (a Year 10 class of 14 year olds). A more detailed version of the work which is presented here in summary form can be found in *The Secondary English Magazine* (Fleming 1997a).

The teacher explains to the pupils the outline of the drama: he will adopt the role of a homeless person; they will interact with his character to find out more about him (using information gained from the objects in his bag and direct questioning); the results will be the basis for their own group work. He then puts on a hat and an old coat, smudges his face with black make-up as he talks to the pupils out of role. The low key approach indicates clearly that the pupils and teacher will collaborate in making the fiction and does not place too much emphasis on the theatricality of the role.

The pupils are invited to invent a scenario which involves all of them and into which the character will be introduced. They decide on a picnic and bring the scene alive by creating simple scenes and conversations which might be taking place. The teacher in role as the homeless person clutching a bag sits some distance from the group and waits for them to notice him and make the first move. When they do so, he is at first withdrawn and reluctant to interact with them but gradually responds to their advances. This appears to be a high risk strategy but the lure of wanting to know more about the character is a strong motivation to make the interaction work. The pupils know there are clues in the bag, but they have to work hard to gain the confidence of the character before he will let them know.

The pupils discover through questioning that the contents of the bag (small Bible, a fragment of a letter, a music box, etc.) provide clues to his past. This is not seeking to be highly realistic; the idea of a homeless person sitting in a park happily discussing the contents of his bag with a group of young people on a picnic may seem a little far-fetched (although people are often eager to disclose their life story to strangers). However, the game format (it resembles a game of 20 questions) and the fact that the pupils have been told in advance the broad parameters sustains the work. This is conducted as a spontaneous, living through drama with pupils and teacher creating the meaning and past life together.

Having established the outline of Charlie Foster's biography the pupils are given the task of creating a significant moment from his life, incorporating one of the objects into the scene which is then presented to the others. The use of the objects as symbols helps the groups to create drama which is focused; the meaning of each individual scene is enriched by being set against the work of the other groups.

These examples will be used to examine the validity of distinguishing between 'performance' and such concepts as 'presenting' and 'showing' but first the emergence of those distinctions in a historical context will be considered.

Performing and presenting

Bolton (1998:16) in his detailed history of drama teaching has described how 'doing away' with an audience has been an important and persistent theme for many drama writers. Harriet Findlay-Johnson saw the need to remove the audience which she did by turning the non-actors into stage-managers or into active commentators or spectators. Slade (1954) took the view that to make children conscious of an audience prematurely was to destroy their own 'child drama'. Way's distinction between drama (linked with experience) and theatre (linked with communication) reinforced this view (1967:3). He believed that any attempt to coerce or impose communication too soon leads to 'artificiality' and ' destroys the value of the intended experience'.

These views are well known and often quoted. However, it is less often acknowledged that Way also gave a somewhat grudging acceptance that sometimes performance was inevitable but should not involve too much of a change from 'drama' to 'theatre'. He used the term 'sharing' rather than 'performing' and drew attention to the way in which the physical relationship between pupils and audience makes a difference.

> Many of the most valuable qualities of drama are retained during the experience of sharing if the shape of the playing area is right – that is on the floor space, with the audience sitting informally around the action.   (Way 1967:281)

For Way it is important that pupils are not suddenly made to perform on a 'picture-frame stage' to a large audience because otherwise they may lose 'the depth of concentration and absorption which can help them to appear in public without loss of the basic qualities of their work'. Here Way seems to acknowledge that given the right context and preparation it is possible to retain 'quality of experience' even in performance.

Pemberton-Billing and Clegg (1965:18) defined theatre as an 'art for showing' and at first they too appear to reject the idea of pupils performing.

> Faced with lines to be read or recited, movements to be remembered and the need for effective projection, the child actor can make little use of his own observations of life, his own speech and movement, or his own way of reacting to situations. He becomes an automaton in the hands of the producer, giving little of his real self to the part ...

However, they express a degree of ambivalence in acknowledging that theatre has some role to play as an extracurricular activity. It is possible to see here a version of what might be termed an 'inclusive' approach to drama.

> This is not to say that theatre is either bad or wrong, but merely that it should not be confused with child drama. Theatre can be a useful and enjoyable out-of-school activity: child drama is an educational medium.   (ibid:19)

Seely (1976:104) too gives voice to what was by now a fairly standard view that

> if we ask children to prepare a scene or sequence deliberately for performance, even if only to the rest of the class, there will be different emphases in the work that is done, and particularly in the form of instruction and discussion.

However, he too is ambivalent about the status of performance, urging caution rather than outright rejection:

> It is important...to remain aware of the precaution that lay behind the drama/theatre distinction: children do not benefit from too much exposure too early, and may even suffer because of it. Particularly when working on expressive improvisation, the teacher must consider very carefully the degree to which children should be exposed to an audience at any particular stage of experience, and work to avoid the pitfalls involved. (ibid:125)

It is clear that Slade's ideas were still very influential in 1970 when Goodridge published *Drama in the Primary School*. She insists that the end product of drama in the primary school should be the experience of it, the process rather than a performance to an audience and quotes the Plowden Report to support her view. 'Though some primary school children enjoy having an audience of other children or their parents, formal representation of plays on a stage is usually out of place' (p.74). While recognising the dangers in performance she acknowledges that sometimes a performance for parents is necessary.

> Communication with an audience in the adult theatre sense cannot be possible with children of this age. Giving a performance usually means that techniques are imposed on the children before they are ready for them and so often the audience has not sufficient understanding or control to behave appropriately. However sometimes it is necessary to offer a programme of work to parents. In this case teachers should keep the occasion as informal and as like ordinary class work as possible without worrying the children with other long drilling rehearsals or last-minute instructions. (p.74)

These comments are not untypical and they show that the frequent assumption that performance and 'theatre' were completely ruled out in 'progressive' drama practice at that time is not entirely true. We find in these comments quoted above a combination of wisdom and naivety. The idea that the quality of the experience is likely to change if a group of pupils is suddenly pushed on to a stage in front of an adult audience is convincing. However, the quotations embody a very traditional model both of theatre and of preparation for performance, involving 'drilling rehearsals' and becoming an 'automaton' in the hands of the producer. Chapter 5 discussed contrasting models of theatre practice and pointed out that the traditional image of the relationship between audience and performer is a fairly late development in the history of the stage (Bennett 1997). The writers on drama quoted above subscribe to a form of essentialism which does not reflect the actual way theatre and performance have variously been conceived. As O'Toole (1992:11) has stated:

> The practice of a director taking a script, blocking it to the writer's instructions, real or assumed and demanding obedience to these constraints from the actors…is now thoroughly discredited.

With the introduction of concepts like 'presenting' (or 'sharing') as opposed to 'performing' it is apparent that the concept of audience is no longer the key factor in distinguishing one form of drama from another. The argument has been advanced that in all forms of drama activity the participants have a sense of audience even if there is no audience present (Robinson 1980:242, Fleming 1994:15). Participants in a whole-group, spontaneous improvisation can be said to form an audience for each others' work. Bolton (1998:259) has stated, contrary to his earlier view expressed in *Towards a Theory of Drama in Education*, that audience is 'a common factor in classroom drama'. He distinguishes between 'presenting' and 'performing' on the basis not of the presence or absence of an audience but in terms of the actor's intention.

> I want to suggest therefore that the term 'performance' in a drama context, is most meaningful when it refers to acting for which an actor would be expected to be applauded and that it be replaced by the term 'presentation' in respect of dramatic activity in which the acting is not highly relevant in itself.   (p.262)

He goes on to suggest that the audience may in part determine how the acting behaviour is to be perceived, 'what was intended by the players as a presentation could be turned by the audience into a performance' (p.263). It is the case therefore that 'acting in its narrowest sense may be determined, not so much by identifiable behaviours, as by the combined intentions of the actors and audience' (p.270).

This distinction is useful in drawing attention to the different 'flavour' which attaches to the different forms of behaviour. One smacks of 'theatricality' and 'show', the other carries connotations of 'depicting significant subject matter for an audience to examine' (p.263). However, the differences are difficult to sustain on the basis of *intentions* whether of the actors or audience. It is as if we have to look 'behind' the external action to see what is there in order to make a judgement. The implication is that an intention is a physical process or state accompanying the acting which somehow determines its quality.

According to Wittgenstein, intention is not determined by thought processes (contrary to what common sense seems to tell us). Intention is similar to meaning in that respect. 'It may seem that meaning something is the act of directing one's attention towards it but no such act need be involved' (Glock 1996:179).

And nothing is more wrong-headed than calling meaning a mental activity! Unless, that is, one is setting out to produce confusion. (It would also be possible to speak of an activity of butter when it rises in price, and if no problems are produced by this it is harmless.)   (Wittgenstein 1953:693)

'Mental or physical processes or states are neither necessary nor sufficient for believing, intending or meaning something' (Glock 1996:179). In the case of the actors how do we determine their intentions? By asking them? They might tell us in advance that they have no intention of trying to win applause but act in a way which makes us say that in fact they are seeking applause. In that case who is correct? Conversely they might state before the performance an intention of winning applause but their acting might make us conclude they had no such intention. They may step on stage with the intention of winning applause but if that thought 'disappears' from their mind how do we judge their intention? As Lyas (1973:195) puts it 'we need to distinguish between what a person explicitly tells us about his intentions...and what we know from his other words and deeds about his intentions'. 'Intention' makes more sense in terms of describing patterns in people's lives than by reference to inner thoughts. To distinguish presenting from performance by reference to intention is simply making a qualitative judgement about the acting behaviour, although language deceives into thinking that there is something else going on called 'intention' which accompanies the acting.

There is a parallel here with the distinction between internal and external dimensions of experience discussed in Chapter 4. It is not a matter of denying the existence of inner states but pointing out that words which appear to describe inner processes (meaning, feeling, intending) get their meaning by virtue of the contexts in which people act. As suggested in Chapter 4 we need to direct our attention away from what accompanies particular activities in drama (in this case intention) towards the context or circumstances in which the drama takes place.

Process and product

The distinction between 'process' and 'product' created false trails in thinking about drama teaching. The assumption that a performance in a theatre to an audience constituted a 'product' and that improvised work in a drama studio amounted to a 'process' does not stand up to scrutiny. As Bolton (1998:261) suggests, it is mistaken to give the impression that 'process' is to be seen as an alternative to 'product' for 'they are interdependent not polar concepts'. In *Starting Drama Teaching* (1994:17) I commented on the distinction as follows:

Pupils are always in their drama, whatever form it takes, working towards a product. In the same way when they are actually engaged in a performance they are involved in a dramatic process. To preserve an exclusive distinction between process and product is sometimes like trying to distinguish between the notion of a football match from playing football; it as if someone denies any ability to talk about the score or to identify the key player of the match on the grounds that they were only involved in the process.

However, what is missing from the distinction given here is the value of the concept of 'process' in directing our attention outwards and 'horizontally' towards the context which gave rise to the work rather than inwards to what is thought to be hidden behind the external actions. The examples which were given at the start of this chapter described three 'products' or 'performances' but the context from which each of these derived is important in understanding its origins, meaning, educational purpose and something of the likely impact on the participants. There is a theoretical and practical point to be made here. Drama in an educational context is different from 'pure' performance (in a traditional sense) because the process or context must always be taken into account when judging the work. When I watch a performance in a theatre the process leading up to the performance matters less to me than the final product I am witnessing; in a drama classroom as suggested in Chapter 4 the process is more important. The practical point is that the quality of experience in performance is likely to be dependent on the teaching process.

The examples of performance given at the beginning of this chapter differed in quality. When the primary age pupils presented their play about the Irish Potato Famine it lost much of its immediacy and content; pupils faltered over words in a way which they had not in the preceding lessons. This was partly a function of their age and experience but it was also related to the complexity and varied activities in the process. In order to present a more polished performance, the project would have required more rehearsal but this was not the priority on this occasion. However the performance of the work had value as a celebration of achievement, a way of unifying the previous activities and of consolidating the learning and understanding gained.

The Royal National Theatre's 'Transformation' artist-in-residency project with primary schools in Tower Hamlets in London culminates each year in a performance. This takes place in a theatre (either the National Theatre itself or the People's Palace in Mile End) and derives from the workshop activities undertaken with the pupils in the different schools. By having the performance as a concrete goal everyone involved (pupils, teachers and workshop leaders) is provided with a source of motivation and common focus. It is also a celebration of achievement and widening of perspective; pupils in each school who have been working independently are able to watch the drama of other pupils who have been working on a similar theme. The performance, however, has a deeper function. It teaches pupils about communication, spatial awareness, audience response and shared values in the context of work on meaningful content. The performance itself is very far removed from any sense of 'showing off' but consciously seeks to encourage communal participation and respect towards the work of others. This work is currently being evaluated by a research team (of which I am a member) led by Professor Peter Tymms at the Curriculum, Evaluation and Management Centre at the University of Durham. For more details of this project see a forthcoming publication by Tamsin Larby.

Theatricality

Finch has suggested that one of the things we can learn from Wittgenstein is 'how profoundly we have to understand something "on the surface" to find the place where theory and practice are united' (Finch 1995:163). Many of the writers on drama quoted in this chapter took the view that certain types of performance (e.g. to a public, external audience) may be inappropriate because they produce the wrong kind of experience. Throughout the history of the teaching of drama writers have expressed reservations about the potential dangers of performance and many of them have set off in search of theoretical distinctions in kind between different types of activities. However, instead of chasing theoretical, 'essentialist' distinctions it is more helpful to think in terms of 'successful' and 'unsuccessful' drama or good and bad teaching.

Warnings about the dangers of what might be termed 'theatricality' are frequently found in writing about the teaching of drama. Findlay-Johnson was concerned to do away with 'acting for display' although she did not comment on any ill-effect 'wrought by the presence of an adult audience of parents and other local villagers' (Bolton 1998:16). Slade (1954:351) was worried that pupils might be turned into 'bombastic little boasters'. Allen (1979:128) referred to the standard, poor performances of nativity plays in primary schools in which the pupils were rarely audible and invariably more intent on making contact with relatives in the audience than focusing on the play. Bolton, in 1981, reiterated the view that he did not want to encourage productions of the kind that require the teacher/director to be 'brilliantly inventive and the performers to be conforming automatons' (Bolton 1981:268). O'Neill and Lambert (1982:25) expressed the view that 'theatre' (which they defined at that time in terms of performance) could result in a 'superficial playing out of events, lacking in seriousness and sometimes accompanied by a certain degree of showing off'.

These are legitimate concerns but such sentiments were not confined to writers on education. Lewicki (1996:21) has pointed out that the educational activities of pioneers in drama coincided with the 'Big Reform' in theatre associated with Stanislavski which amounted to a search for a more authentic style of acting. Just a year after Way published *Development Through Drama* (1967) Roose-Evans (1968) published *Directing a Play* in which he described his approach to directing *Under Milk Wood*.

> In rehearsal a great deal of improvisation was used in order to open up the individual characterisations. The entire cast was always present at these sessions sharing, as it were, in the community's collective memories (many of the improvisations showed the various characters at different stages of their lives).
>
> (p.11)

Even though Slade and Way were very much involved in the theatre, the lack of communication between drama in the context of education and in the professional theatre concealed points of contact and of potential mutual enrichment.

As well as describing his departure from a very traditional model of rehearsal, Roose-Evans (p.93) also made the simple but telling point that, 'no amount of true feeling will compensate an audience for inaudibility'. When preparing for a public performance it is clear that the emphasis will be different from simply sharing work in the course of a drama workshop. This is not an argument against performance, it is simply to point out that priorities can change when a play has to be polished for public presentation. There is no *necessary* connection, however, between public performance and any lack of understanding or superficiality.

Drama seems to hover ambiguously between the sublime and the superficial. On the one hand it is potentially a rich source of learning and insight, life-enhancing and inspirational. On the hand many writers have recognised that it can take a hollow form reinforcing all the wrong kinds of personal traits and characteristics. Its imagery can be used in very negative ways. 'Staginess' is hardly a term of approval; we refer pejoratively to someone as being 'a bit of an actor'. The 'luvvie' phenomenon in the theatre is easily prone to satire.

This negative or ambiguous view of drama is not new, nor has art in general been always embraced as something positive. Plato in *The Republic* mounted a well-known attack on drama and this theme has been repeated at different times in its history. According to Young (1992:303), Neitzsche's view of art was also ambivalent:

> At some stages in his career he sees art as, literally, a life-saving activity, our only salvation from 'nausea and suicide'. At others, he sees it as useless, hostile even, to the promotion of life.

In the *The Birth of Tragedy* Neitzsche defined two competing but complementary impulses in Greek culture – the Apollonian and Dionysian.

> The Apollonian takes its name from Apollo, the god of light, dream, and prophecy, while the Dionysian takes its name from Dionysus, the god of intoxication. Apollo is associated with visible form, rational knowledge, and

moderation, Dionysius with formless flux, mysticism and excess.

(Smith 2000:xvi)

In artistic terms Apollo is associated with the plastic or representational arts of painting and sculpture while Dionysius is the god of music, the art which is essentially 'non representational and without physical form' (ibid:xvi). Dionysian art is associated with a 'surging energy unleashed in anarchic ways, impulse alike to creativity and destruction' while Apollonian art is associated with the 'ordering of logical thought and faith in reason' (Blake *et al.* 2000:96). Although these metaphors were first used to describe different art forms they can be applied to drama. In this context an excess of Appollian influence 'gradually overgrows its Dyonisian regions and must necessarily drive it to self annihilation; to the lethal plunge into bourgeois theatre' (Neitzsche 2000:78 (first published in 1872)). Great art requires a fusion of both.

> The Appollonian and Dionysian drives are, however, as complementary as they are antagonistic, and it is the shifting balance of their combination which produces the ultimate art of Greek tragedy. Without the other to hold it in check, each drive would tend to the extreme. Unrestrained by the Dionysian, the Appollonian produces the secular and militaristic culture of ancient Rome, concerned simply with the imposition of form and discipline. Without the counterbalance of the Appollonian, the Dionysian results in ... pessimism and passivity.
>
> (Smith 2000)

Parallels can be made with these two concepts and the phenomenon of 'theatricality'. The instinctive to 'show off' is not just a matter of the individual's personal growth (or lack of it) but affects the aesthetic impact of the drama; it serves to distract from meaning and truth rather than reveal it. The understanding of human experience which a play offers us lies not in the dormant text but in its realisation in performance; a bad performance can obscure rather than reveal insight. An excess of the Apollonian influence in drama teaching leads to the kind of authoritarian directing to which so many writers objected, an excess of logic and structure over experience and meaning. Drama in education injected an element of Dionysian energy into the drama teaching world.

Blake *et al.* (2000:96) draw parallels between the notion of 'theatricality' which they draw from Nietzshe's thinking and what is happening more generally in education at the present time.

> Just as the excessive influence of the Apollonian led to the degeneration of tragedy into what Neitzshe calls bourgeois theatre, so we argue has a similar theatricisation occurred in education: standards and values have now become flickering shadows of what they might be. Practice has become contrived and self conscious, staged and presented as the object of accountability's gaze.

The theatre imagery can be extended. OFSTED inspections force schools and teachers into stage-management, into presenting a false image and concealing the truth. 'Performance management', as the term suggests, seeks to improve 'performance' without necessarily paying attention to values and content.

Performance then is a key element in drama but it needs to be directed at revealing the truth. Slade and Way were against showing off. Later drama practitioners were not only against showing off but were against the lack of attention to content and meaning which they saw as an inevitable result of performing. They also believed that performing could not induce the right kind of feeling. But we need to see these as contingent and not necessary aspects of performing; there are good and bad performances. As Wittgenstein would have put it, we have been digging too deep, trying to look behind the actions instead of looking on the surface.

We can return now to the 'stool pigeon' lesson in the BBC film of Heathcote's work which was described in Chapter 4. It is a useful example because of its interesting history. When it was first published it was widely interpreted as a piece of spontaneous, improvised drama but it later turned out that the sequence had been more planned than this (Davis 1985, Morgan and Saxton 1987:24, Bolton 1998:221).

> When for instance the 'Stool Pigeon' breaks down and weeps, this appears to be a remarkable moment of natural spontaneous expression of emotion (some might be led to think epitomising Heathcote's work at its best). It was, however, a piece of contrivance between an astute film director and the boy actor who had previously raised the question with Heathcote and the class whether it would be appropriate for his character to cry. Likewise the deft hiding of the keys when the guards suddenly arrive, had been worked out technically ready for the camera to 'make authentic'.   (Bolton 1998:221)

When Heathcote first confronted the pupils in her teacher in role as a guard they shot her. This is not shown on film; instead they interact with her in a tense dramatic moment. How reassured many young drama teachers would have been in the 1970s to have known about the drama 'going wrong' the first time round! The point here is not to debunk this film or to suggest that the emperor has no clothes. Heathcote herself made no claims about this lesson nor sought to misrepresent it because she had a deeper understanding of what she was about than many of her followers. The contextual information however does help us to reinterpret the drama. I made the point in *Starting Drama Teaching* (1994:16) that this film, famous for advancing the cause of experiential, living through drama, could be equally judged as an effective piece of theatre. I would go further now and suggest that it counts as a very effective piece of rehearsed performance. Some commentators have objected to my use of the term 'rehearsed' in relation to this work but I would suggest that is because the word conjures up the wrong kinds of images (based on a traditional model). We can just as easily use the word 'rehearsed' in relation to this piece of work and suggest that Heathcote was pioneering a sophisticated form of rehearsal.

We can also analyse this work not so much as 'living through drama' but as the construction and communication of meaning through the use of signs. Much of the preparation for the scene was taken up with building self-spectatorship in all the boys and a 'rational examination of how people like guards signal power' (Bolton 1998:221). At the climax to the drama the teacher is watching from the side with the other spectators. It is ironic, in the light of the emphasis on process in drama in education practice, that what was presented in this film and left for posterity was a product. Much of the all important process was left on the cutting room floor.

CHAPTER 8

Drama and language: meaning and logic

In Act 2, scene 2 of Brian Friel's play *Translations*, set in Ireland in the 1830s, Yolland and Maire have left a dance hand in hand and are now alone. At first they appear to be communicating normally:

> MAIRE: O my God, that leap across the ditch nearly killed me.
> YOLLAND: I could scarcely keep up with you.
> MAIRE: Wait till I get my breath back.
> YOLLAND: We must have looked as if we were being chased.

However the audience is soon reminded that they do not in fact speak each other's languages. Maire speaks Irish and has so far only learned one or two words of English. This is highlighted when they coincidentally say virtually the same thing to each other without understanding what the other is saying.

> MAIRE: The grass must be wet. Me feet are soaking.
> YOLLAND: Your feet must be wet. The grass is soaking.

This exchange is reminiscent of Beckett or Pinter; two people exchanging words without any real communication, except that here the reason is rather different; it is the lack of a shared language between the two which is causing the problem. One of the play's conventions is that the Irish speaking characters actually speak in English so that the audience can understand what they are saying. When Maire speaks in this exchange the audience must 'hear' Irish.

She remembers a few words of English, including a single sentence which her aunt Mary taught her. This becomes a source of humour because Yolland's reaction (derived from the fact that she has inadvertently made a connection with his family background) makes her think she may have said 'something dirty'.

> MAIRE: Shhh (*she holds her hand up for silence – she is trying to remember her one line of English. Now she remembers it and she delivers the line as if English were her language – easily, fluidly, conversationally.*)
> George, 'In Norfolk we besport ourselves around the maypoll.' (*sic*)
> YOLLAND: Good God do you? That's where my mother comes from – Norfolk.

Norwich actually. Not exactly Norwich town but a small village called Little Walsingham close beside it. But in our own village of Winfarthing we have a maypole too and every year on the first of May – (He stops abruptly, only now realising. He stares at her. She in turn misunderstands his excitement.)

MAIRE: *(To herself)* Mother of God, my aunt Mary wouldn't have taught me something dirty, would she?

(Pause, YOLLAND extends his hand to MAIRE. She turns away from him and moves slowly across the stage.)

It is now Yolland's turn to try to overcome the barrier to communication by searching for some words to which she might respond. The only words of Irish which he has learned so far are place names. He tries one name, first softly and tentatively, looking for a sound to which she might respond. She stops, listens, turns towards him and speaks.

(They are now facing each other and begin moving – almost imperceptibly towards one another.)

MAIRE: Carraig an Phoill.

YOLLAND: Carraig na Ri Loch na nEan.

MAIRE: Loch an Inubhair. Machaire Buidhe.

YOLLAND: Machaire Mor. Cnoc na Mona.

MAIRE: Cnoc na nGabhar.

YOLLAND: Mullach.

MAIRE: Port.

YOLLAND: Tor.

MAIRE: Lag.

(She holds out her hands to YOLLAND. He takes them. Each now speaks almost to himself/herself.)

YOLLAND: I wish to God you could understand me.

MAIRE: Soft hands; a gentleman's hands.

The exchange in Irish is reminiscent of the kind of drama exercise described in Chapter 6 when two participants are asked to conduct a conversation using just a single word or an arbitrary choice of words such as the days of the week. Expression, tone, non-verbal signs and context help to convey meaning. It is in some senses a celebration of the art form of drama which makes use of a complex and interconnected set of signs other than just language. The exchange both highlights the limitations of language but also celebrates its possibilities. Language is both 'intelligible and sensuous' (Bowie 1990:147). In this case the choice of words is given more poignancy because of the wider context of the play.

Translations is set in 1830's Ireland when the British Army carried out an ordnance survey of the country, changing and Anglicising all the place names.

Yolland is one of the soldiers charged with the job. His task is to take each of the Gaelic names, 'every hill, stream, rock, even every patch of ground which possessed its own distinctive Irish name' and Anglicise it, either by changing it into its approximate English sound or by translating it into English words. The play at one level can be seen as symbolising the death of the Irish language and showing 'the connection between language (its loss and mastery) and politics (its violence and its authority)' (Deane 1996:21). The act of renaming can be seen as a form of cultural imperialism and oppression. The friendly attitude of the British soldiers at the start of the play changes when Yolland goes missing; the British commanding officer threatens to shoot all livestock and to begin evicting and levelling all the houses.

However, to see the play as being only about oppression and dispossession is to miss some of its subtlety and impact as a work of art. An ambiguity in attitude to language is expressed in the character of Maire who wants to learn English so that she can travel to America. 'We should all be learning to speak English. That's what my mother says. That's what I say. That's what Dan O'Connell said last month in Ennis.' Pine (1990:149), in an account of the historical background of the play, points out that nationalists had polarised views about the Irish language. He quotes O'Connell:

> 'Although the Irish language is connected with many recollections that twine round the hearts of Irishmen, yet the superior utility of the English tongue, as the medium of all modern communication, is so great that I can witness without a sigh the gradual disuse of the Irish.'

An element of ambiguity is again reinforced by the fact that Owen, the son of the local schoolmaster, is helping the soldiers in their task of renaming. It would be too simple to see him as just a collaborator who betrays his people. He shows little conscious awareness of the negative implications of his actions. The play is as much (or even more) to do with language, meaning and individual identity as it is about politics and imperialism. The ordnance survey and renaming is seen as a piece of simple logic by the soldiers, a piece of rational, crisp, orderly and efficient restructuring. It is seen as a 'military operation'. The mapping is a metaphor for a process whereby a rich and textured culture is reduced to two dimensions through a quest for certainty and standardisation. (This is not dissimilar to what is happening in education in England and elsewhere.)

> MANUS: There was nothing uncertain about what Lancey said: it's a bloody military operation, Owen! And what's Yolland's function? What's incorrect about the place-names we have here?
> OWEN: Nothing at all. They're just going to be standardised.
> MANUS: You mean changed into English?
> OWEN: Where there's ambiguity, they'll be Anglicised.

The project is described to the locals by Lancey in arid, technical terms.

> 'His Majesty's government has ordered the first ever comprehensive survey of this entire country – a general triangulation which will embrace detailed hydrographic and topographic information and which will be executed to a scale of six inches to the English mile.'

The whole project is based on the assumption that language is simply a process of naming. Yolland is described as one who 'gives names to places'. The quest is for 'up-to-date and accurate information'. Efficiency, effectiveness and 'performativity' are to the fore (see Chapter 3). Language has meaning 'on the surface'. According to Owen it is only necessary to name a thing and 'bang! it leaps into existence'. The character of Hugh embodies the contrasting attitude which sees language in a more complex way, deriving meaning in relation to particular cultural contexts. 'English,' he says, 'couldn't really express us.' It is Hugh who acknowledges the contingency of language,

> 'it is not the literal past, the "facts" of history, that shape us, but images of the past embodied in language.'

Ironically it is Owen who gives voice to a sentiment which has considerable significance in the play as a whole, 'Uncertainty in meaning is incipient poetry.' Owen does not apply the full implications of that insight into the task he is undertaking. It is in fact Yolland who starts to see the truth about what they are doing in their mapping project.

> OWEN: We're making a six-inch map of the country. Is there something sinister in that?
> YOLLAND: Not in –
> OWEN: And we're taking place-names that are riddled with confusion and –
> YOLLAND: Who's confused? Are the people confused?
> OWEN – and we're standardising those names as accurately and as sensitively as we can.
> YOLLAND: Something is being eroded.

It is Yolland who starts to see that language is deeply rooted in culture and as an outsider simply learning the language will not guarantee acceptance in the community.

> YOLLAND: Even if I did speak Irish I'd always be an outsider here, wouldn't I? I may learn the password but the language of the tribe will always elude me, won't it? The private core will always be … hermetic, won't it?

Two contrasting views of language are presented in the play. One is logical, referential and straightforward. Language has meaning by attaching names to objects so that it is simply a matter of efficient organisation to make any changes thought necessary. The alternative is to see language in a richer, more organic way, embedded in cultural contexts. When Hugh at the end of the play agrees to teach Maire English he asks her not to expect too much.

> 'I will provide you with the available words and the available grammar. But will that help you to interpret between privacies? I have no idea. But it's all we have.'

Hugh is referring here not to 'individual' but to 'cultural' privacies. He recognises the demands of the modern world: 'he is willing to aid – he bestows his will upon – those frightened children like Maire who need to learn a new song, in order to recapture faith' (Pine 1990:176). The imagery in the play echoes philosophical explanations about language. These have been recurring themes in this book which will now be explored in more detail.

Language and logic

Language has already figured fairly prominently as a theme in this book. The focus has not been so much on the value of drama in developing language (which is the more common concern in books about drama) but in examining ways in which perspectives on language and meaning can inform theory and practice. This section will examine some of those background ideas in more detail, returning to some of the themes which have been examined in earlier chapters.

Many writers have addressed issues related to what might be described fairly loosely as the relationship between language and reality, a theme common to much postmodern and poststructuralist writing. The work of Wittgenstein however is particularly illuminating because his earlier writing provides an account of some of the thinking which his later writing was to reject. It was pointed out in Chapter 2 that much of the philosophical writing on language was being directed at older ideas and if transported unthinkingly into everyday discourse and practice is likely to cause problems. The retreat into different forms of naive relativism in some postmodernist writing has arisen partly for that reason. A brief examination of the tradition from which Wittgenstein was departing will therefore help throw light on the radical insights brought by his later philosophy.

There is danger in the discussion which follows of providing either too much detail so that the focus becomes obscured or too little detail to do justice to the central ideas. Numerous books and articles have been written about Wittgenstein, reinterpreting his work, contesting earlier interpretations and challenging what others have written. However, not to address some of his thinking in a more systematic way than simply a passing quotation would be to miss an opportunity to highlight the relevance of his thinking to contemporary education in general and drama teaching in particular. It has been a theme of this book that Wittgenstein, for all his reputation for theoretical obscurity, has much relevance to the theory and practice of drama teaching.

Wittgenstein's early philosophy is described in the *Tractatus*, the only work published in his life time. It consists of seven major propositions each with numbered sub-sections; the whole book is logical and ordered in an elaborate structure that reflects its subject matter. Wittgenstein developed in the *Tractatus* a picture theory of meaning. In other words he sought to show a correspondence between language and the world in terms of the common structures they share. Underlying this goal was the view that because we use language to talk about the world, it must be related to the world in a strict logical fashion, there must be a logical correspondence between language and what it represents.

Language consists of propositions which are made up of names. Similarly the world consists of 'facts' which are made up of objects. Grayling (1996:29) summarises his views as follows:

> The objects, which are the ultimate constituents of the world, are denoted by the ultimate constituents of language, the names; names combine to form elementary propositions, which correspond to states of affairs; and each of these further combine to form, respectively, propositions and the facts which, in a sense to be explained, those propositions 'picture'.

The metaphor of map making in *Translations* is appropriate here. The map corresponds to, or mirrors, the world in a logical way. Lancey describes the map as a 'representation on paper – a picture'. In the same way language represents reality in strict, logical, isomorphic (one to one) way. Finch (1995:149) describes Wittgenstein's approach in the *Tractatus* as a 'method of abstraction'. In doing so he links him with a tradition in philosophy which increasingly, through its use of formal signs, cut off mathematics, logic and scientific theory from the 'natural, the cultural and the traditional' (ibid:150). For the purposes of this discussion perhaps the flavour and texture of Wittgenstein's quest and solution is as important as a detailed understanding of the intricacies of his arguments. His account of language is of something logical, precise, a kind of 'calculus'; what can be said at all can be said clearly, and 'what we cannot speak about we must pass over in silence' (Wittgenstein 1961:74). It is a distinctively formalist view. Finch has stated that Wittgenstein's early philosophy 'made a god out of rigor or exactitude' (ibid:20).

Language and meaning

Peters and Marshall (1999:28) describe Wittgenstein's quest in his early writing as one which sought for a form of 'logical purity'. They quote from Eagleton's novel

Saints and Scholars which captures in literary, symbolic form the moment of insight that motivated Wittgenstein to change his thinking.

> One day a friend took his photograph on the steps of the Senate House and Wittgenstein asked him where to stand. 'Oh roughly there,' the friend replied, casually indicating a spot. Wittgenstein went back to his room, lay on the floor and writhed in excitement. *Roughly there.* The phrase had opened a world to him. Not 'two inches to the left of that stone, but "roughly there"'. Human life was a matter of roughness, not of precise measurement. Why had he not understood this? He had tried to purge language of its ambiguities....Looseness and ambiguity were not imperfections, they were what made things work.
>
> (Eagleton 1987:42)

The quotation from Augustine which opens the *Philosophical Investigations* embodies the 'common sense' view of language which he now challenges. Augustine describes how he learned language as a child, 'When they (my elders) named some object, accordingly moved towards something, I saw this and I grasped that the thing was called by the sound they uttered when they meant to point it out.' Wittgenstein thought this account was too simple for two major reasons. It treated all language as names which is clearly not the case. But more importantly, even in the case of names, Wittgenstein saw that meaning arises through use, through agreements in culture or 'forms of life' not just by attaching names to objects or phenomena in the world. The idea that language has meaning in a form of life is in total contrast to the idea of language simply as a system of signs. It emphasises instead that language is embedded in the significant behaviour (including non-linguistic behaviour) of human beings.

Wittgenstein's often quoted notion of language games and family resemblances are part of his acceptance of 'blurred concepts as being wholly workable in ordinary life without needing the underpinning of total exactness (unless this has to be *constructed* for some specific purpose)' (Finch 1995:36). The history of much western philosophy can be seen in Wittgenstein's terms as an attempt to detach language from its everyday employment and create problems where previously none had existed.

Wittgenstein was much preoccupied in his writing with what he saw as false dichotomies which dominated earlier philosophical writing such as that between subjectivity and objectivity, mind and body, inner and outer experience. His work demonstrates that the choices which language seems to present to us are in fact false ones derived from a particular misguided view of the way language has meaning. The freedom from the tyranny of language which his writing offers has relevance to theoretical and practical questions because it makes it clear that there is no imperative to choose between competing concepts or to assume that words which appear referential are always necessarily so. We have the term 'drama in education' and we try, unsuccessfully, to define a set of practices to correspond to that term.

Wittgenstein's view of the purpose of philosophy was not 'to impose an order through theory, but to discover the connections which already exist through observation' (Genova 1995:33).

Many of the traditional arguments about drama teaching derive from particular definitions of concepts. The fact that concepts do not have clearly defined boundaries but relate through a process of 'family resemblances' has consequences for drama.

> Consider for example the proceedings that we call 'games'. I mean board-games, card-games, ball-games, Olympic games, and so on. What is common to them all? – Don't say: There must be something common, or they would not be called 'games' – but *look and see* whether there is anything common to all. – For if you look at them you will not see something that is common to all.
>
> (Wittgenstein 1953:66)

It is not necessary to seek for one single definition of 'drama' which can be applied in all cases nor to assume that a term can be used to mean whatever one wants it to mean (a not uncommon misinterpretation of the family resemblance view). It is important to be alert to the fact that demarcating concepts in particular ways may be misleading or useful depending on the specific context. As Wittgenstein says 'we can draw a boundary' but we do not need to discover any such boundary to make the concept 'usable' (ibid:69). For example, when making decisions about whether drama should belong with other art forms, much misplaced energy was expended in debating whether there must be a characteristic which is common to all the arts and distinct from all other areas. However, it not necessary to establish such defining characteristics to be able to use the concepts comfortably; it is enough to recognise that drama more resembles music than physics but that there may be reasons other than ones related to definitions for wanting drama to remain separate as a curriculum subject. Essentialist definitions of 'drama as an art form' or 'drama for learning' at one time prevented some teachers from importing useful techniques into their lessons (mime, movement, dance) because these were considered to be 'not drama'. Arguments in favour of placing theatre practice at the core of a drama curriculum help to highlight the public and cultural aspects of the subject but may result in restricted forms of practice if a narrow definition of theatre is employed. The view that the dramatic art form is only manifest in public products hinges on a definition of 'dramatic art' which smuggles in the conclusion by virtue of the way the initial terms are defined.

Such examples point to the need not so much to define terms but rather to look to the way they are more commonly used and the consequences of drawing boundaries in particular ways, 'for a special purpose' (ibid:69). The relationship between 'drama' and 'play' has importance in the history of drama. The movement away from dramatic playing has meant that exponents have looked less to psychological theories of child play and more to writers on theatre and semiotics for theoretical underpinning for their work. The change of emphasis can be summarised as a move from a 'personal' to a more 'cultural' justification for drama which to some degree parallels the move from logic to culture in Wittgenstein's explanation of meaning.

The cultural justification for drama takes the view that the purpose of teaching is to induct pupils into a community, what Wittgenstein might describe as a context for creating meaning or a web of practices. One way of looking at education is to see it as an initiation into a 'form of life' (Smeyers and Marshall 1995:17). Wittgenstein did not give precise examples of what he meant by this concept but he associated it with the notion of a language game which emphasises the fact that 'the speaking of language is part of an activity...' (Wittgenstein 1953:23). McGinn (1997:51) offers the following helpful explanation:

> The idea of language as a form of life, like the idea of a language game, is to be set over against the idea of language as an abstract system of signs; it again serves to bring into prominence the fact that language is embedded within a horizon of significant, non-linguistic behaviour. Thus, just as the term 'language game' is meant to evoke the idea of language in use within the non-linguistic activities of speakers, so the term 'form of life' is intended to evoke the idea that language and linguistic exchange are embedded in the significantly structured lives of active human agents.

Despite an element of uncertainty attached to interpreting precisely what Wittgenstein meant by the term 'form of life', it can be usefully extended to drama because it implies that pupils need to be initiated into a practice which has its own rules, customs and conventions. The use of such general terms as this avoids the assumption that a cultural justification for drama necessarily equates with one particular form of practice. It could as easily embrace 'process' drama as traditional performance work; the important aspect is that pupils are initiated into forms of knowledge (including for example drama conventions) which are in some sense external to them. On the other hand, the personal justification for drama is based more on what is 'given', and recognises that children have a natural propensity for dramatic playing which needs to be nurtured. As suggested in Chapter 5, the developmental model alone is inappropriate because it does not give an adequate conception of education or teaching.

These two ways of justifying drama are common in the history of drama teaching and as with other dichotomies are often placed in opposition to each other or, more commonly in recent years, brushed aside as being dead issues. But Wittgenstein has useful observations to make when faced with propositions which appear to exclude each other (e.g. drama is 'play' and 'not play'). Logic suggests that a proposition cannot be both true and false at the same time (the law of excluded middle) but language is not rule-bound in that simple way.

The law of excluded middle says here: It must look like this, or like that. So it really – and this is a truism – says nothing at all, but gives us a picture. And the problem ought not to be: does reality accord with the picture or not? And this picture seems to determine what we have to do, what to look for, and how – but it does not do so, just because we do not know how it is to be applied. Here saying 'There is no third possibility' or 'But there can't be a third possibility!' express our inability to turn our eyes away from this picture...

(Wittgenstein 1953:352)

There are a number of other consequences which arise from this view of language and meaning which have already appeared in this book in a number of chapters. It prevents us from trying to see behind the external actions of the drama to identify its quality in relation to individual feelings or intentions. Peters and Marshall (1999:27) describe Wittgenstein's later thought as distinctively postmodern in that it no longer clings to the idea that 'something remains hidden – a crystalline, pure logical essence – that directs our thought, language and culture'. His views helps us to see that trying to formulate a definitive theory of drama by establishing an overarching metalanguage or metanarrative is mistaken – such a theory would escape from under the language which attempted to enclose it.

Wittgenstein's view of language also helps us to see past the problem of 'objectivity' in relation for example to assessment which has exercised many writers.

Wittgenstein is no longer bothered by an 'objectivity' that lies outside of all language, culture and human norms, one that is supposed to set the standard for all truth and meaning. Objectivity is now a product of human agreement in language and actions. (If we persist in thinking that in this account 'something is missing', it may be because we have not yet caught a glimpse of the sufficiency, completeness, and ungroundedness of sense-making language.)

(Finch 1995: 122)

There is an implicit assumption in much current educational policy and practice that to solve the problem of objectivity in assessment there is a necessity to get the language of criteria and descriptors right. So we get ever more complex lists, structures and definitions which try to pin down meaning exactly. There is a naivety in the proliferation of competencies and standards for assessing student teachers, as if there could be any common understanding of what reaching a standard means simply through adopting a common language. How for example do we interpret a standard like 'set high expectation for pupils' behaviour'? If we begin to unpack the statement and to share interpretations through examples we inevitably get into the business of comparing values and priorities. Language is learned and only has meaning in a culture or community of practices so assessment can only properly operate through action and sharing judgements, not just through exchanging criteria in forms of words.

Perhaps most importantly Wittgenstein's view of language and meaning provides an insight into concepts such as 'feeling' and 'understanding' which have provided many difficulties in the history of drama teaching. To the questions 'what is feeling?' 'what is understanding?' the appropriate answer is that they are words. That seems at first to be either extremely naive or an obstinate piece of question begging but the insight dissolves some of the problems with these concepts. Chapter 6 discussed the negative consequences of interpreting understanding as an event (or even more misguided as a mental event); understanding is not an 'all or nothing affair'. It was suggested that surface learning (for example learning words by heart) may be an important part of a journey towards deeper forms of learning. Consideration was also given to the way in which our understanding of 'feeling' hinges on its use in language, a discussion which will be extended in Chapter 9.

Attention to language and meaning also resolves problems associated with the concept of the 'self' in relation to drama. This is easy to misunderstand and sometimes is misunderstood when it is assumed that the word 'private' is being used here in its normal sense. What Wittgenstein abolished was the notion of an absolutely private self. It is not for example a matter of contrasting private thoughts and values which people *choose* to keep to themselves. The private/public dichotomy is sometimes wrongly expressed in these terms. As Finch (1995:86) says:

> To get rid of the metaphysically private self, not to think or experience the world in that way any more, is actually to strike a blow in favor of genuine (i.e. relative) privacy. The former is a prison, the latter is a choice.

The focus for Wittgenstein's main attack on the metaphysical private self is provided by his argument against a private language. A private language is one whose words 'refer to what can only be known to the person speaking: to his immediate private sensations' (1953:243). Could we, he asks,

> imagine a language in which a person could write down or give vocal expression to his inner experiences – his feelings, moods and the rest – for his private use? Well, can't we do so in our ordinary language? But that is not what I mean. The individual words of this language are to refer to what can only be known to the person speaking; to his immediate private sensations. So another person cannot understand the language.   (ibid:243)

Such a language would only be possible if words acquire meaning simply by being linked to private experiences. One of the objections to the possibility of a private language is that there would be no guarantee of consistency in using the language. In order for that to happen criteria of correctness or rules are required which arise in contexts of agreement *between* people. The argument rests on the fact that language has meaning largely in external public contexts.

The self grows and forms 'outwards' rather than 'inwards'. We define ourselves in relation to others, in terms of the language we use. Drama is essentially a social and dialogic activity – meaning is negotiated on the surface. It is legitimate to say that drama is about understanding the self and our relationship to the world as long as we see in those terms the public nature of meaning. 'We make sense of our lives, feelings, and attitudes by seeing how my purported feelings, attitudes, hopes, and so forth position me within the grammar of the public language that I have learned' (ibid: 201).

Language and drama

Drama as an art form brings some of these truths about language and meaning more to the surface. Language in drama is more obviously not about externalising inner thoughts but about creating meaning between people. The power of drama as an art form derives in part from the fact that it does not operate through 'conceptual access to possible worlds' but through 'physical access'. In other words the 'constructed world' is 'shown' to the audience' (Elam 1988:111). Although the sign systems of drama are complex, it is language which is usually most immediately present to the audience. The drama does not relate to the real world on the basis of simple representation or picturing (the *Tractatus* view of language and meaning) but in more complex ways which affect the uses of language.

A naturalistic drama gives the impression that language is being employed in exactly the same way that it would in real life. There are important differences however. More often than not the context for communication has to be established by the words spoken by the characters. That is why overuse of narration in children's drama should be avoided because it tends to move the activity away from the dramatic genre towards narrative. The opening dialogue of *Translations* and the exchange of words establishes just enough context for the communication to take place; more contextual details unfold as the scene develops. We are introduced to characters we have never met before. We do not yet know who they are or what their signifcance will be in the play.

> MANUS: We're doing very well. And we're going to try it once more – just once more. Now – relax and breathe in . . . deep . . . and out . . . in . . . and out.
> (SARAH *shakes her head vigorously and stubbornly.*)
> MANUS: Come on, Sarah. This is our secret.
> (*Again vigorous and stubborn shaking of* SARAH's *head.*)
> MANUS: Nobody's listening. Nobody hears you.

JIMMY: 'Ton d'embeit epeita thea glaukopis Athene.'

MANUS: Get your tongue and your lips working. 'My name – " ' Come on. One more try. 'My name is " ' Good girl.

SARAH: My

MANUS: Great. 'My name – " '

SARAH: My . . . . . my . . . . .

MANUS: Raise your head, Shout it out. Nobody's listening.

JIMMY: 'All hekelos estai en Atreidao domois…'

MANUS: Jimmy, please! Once more – just once more – 'My name – " ' Good girl. Come on now. Head up. Mouth open.

We find a 'dynamic world already in progress' (Elam 1988:140). This is reinforced by the use of personal pronouns which establishes a key element of drama: that life is being lived out in front of us in action and not reported in narrative. It is established that Manus is trying to teach Sarah to speak but the significance of this to the wider theme of the play is not yet apparent. The interventions in Greek by Jimmy also do not yet have any significance. As members of the audience however we know that the meaning which will be established does not exist outside the world of the play but will evolve as the drama develops.

In process drama the meaning of particular components of the work (e.g. small group play making) does not exist independently of the rest of the work. This was true of the examples of performance given at the beginning of the last chapter. The work on the Stevie Smith poem *Not Waving But Drowning* was not self-contained but related to the drama created by other groups. This was also true of the drama based on the teacher in role as a homeless person and the work on the Irish potato famine. In each case the particular presentations related to a broader context created in the workshop activities. This is a common and valuable way of working. However, pupils (particularly those who are more experienced in drama) need to have the experience of creating a drama which is self-contained in which the meaning is unfolded as the play develops. Only in this way will they be asked to think about exposition in their own creative work, which is an important element of dramatic art.

In the past I have argued, along with other writers, that drama is valuable for language development because it provides rich contexts for pupils to use different registers. The fictitious context can provide protection while the use of language is extended. That view still holds. However, there is an even more fundamental reason for seeing the importance of drama with respect to language not just in relation to its development but in terms of values, attitudes and understanding. Participation in drama (as creator or spectator) is to engage with the construction of meaning in a way which acknowledges context, culture and values. Drama helps us not to take meaning for granted, to look underneath surface meanings and explore differences.

Drama and literacy

It is for this reason that drama exists as an important antidote to the utilitarian excesses of the literacy strategy recently introduced into primary and secondary schools in England. Here language is to be plundered for what it can yield in terms of its technical content. Form and structure are dominant. When trying to prepare a unit of work for the literacy hour based on the poem *The Highwayman* (described in Chapter 5) I was struck by a description in McCourt's *Angela's Ashes* of the way the young Frank responds to the poem. A verse is recited to him each day while he is in hospital by a young girl, Patricia, who dies before she reaches the end of the poem:

> Every day I can't wait for the doctors and nurses to leave me alone so I can learn a new verse from Patricia and find out what's happening to the highwayman and the landlord's red-lipped daughter. I love the poem because it is exciting. The redcoats are after the highwayman because they know he told her, 'I'll come to thee by moonlight, though hell should bar the way'.

I came across a commercial publication linking the poem with the literacy hour in which the content of the former is largely ignored and the pupils have to set about plundering its verses for spellings, examples of rhythms and literary devices such as onomatopoeia and metaphor without any real appreciation of how content and form relate to create meaning. Inevitably the framework document itself recognises that teachers should aim for 'high levels of motivation and active engagement of pupils' (DfEE:8). The emphasis on text as well as on word and sentence level is intended to retain focus on meaning. However the explicit message here runs counter to the sub-text contained in the presentation of the strategy in which logic and rationality are dominant with lists, objectives and structures and with content subordinate to form.

> Once the zealots of the new literacy can break reading down into a matter of orchestrating a full range of reading cues (phonic, graphic, syntactic, contextual), knowing grapheme/phoneme correspondences, tracking the text in the right order, page by page, left to right, top to bottom; pointing while reading/telling a story – then their task is done. Literacy is taken apart and spread out for inspection, like the engine of a car dismantled and displayed on the garage floor. This is not to say that these things may not be valuable to learn. The point is crucial. It may well be useful (and interesting) to know grapheme/phoneme correspondences. But to say this is very different from foregrounding these skills, as skills, in a conception of literacy.
>
> (Blake *et al.* 2000:93)

It is a curious truth that responses to the literacy hour among teachers are very varied and do not divide along conventional 'traditional' and progressive' beliefs.

It seems to be welcomed and castigated by teachers in almost equal numbers and with different views about education and language. The reason is that the strategy itself, like the National Curriculum, neither guarantees nor inhibits good teaching. It is merely a 'script' ready to be animated and enlivened in the classroom in which knowledge about language can be properly integrated with the excitement of reading and studying literature.

Literature of course draws attention to the lack of transparency in language (in contrast to the functional lists in the strategy) but drama has a particular role to play because it more closely ressembles 'real life'. The degree to which drama does and does not represent the real world will be discussed in the next chapter.

CHAPTER 9

Drama and aesthetics: expression and representation

The drama which each group of mixed age pupils is about to perform to the rest of the class has a common theme. Each presentation depicts the visit of a teenage foreign visitor to a family in England as a part of an educational exchange. Several of the groups begin their performance by having the foreign visitor (played by a pupil) articulate their version of what happened during the visit in a brief monologue. This is followed by a depiction of the events as they actually happened. The content of the drama focuses on very simple, everyday situations with no obvious apparent dramatic content: doing homework, watching television, mealtimes, going to a football match. In each case, however, the visitor is inadvertently made to feel uncomfortable in some way which creates an extra, subtle layer of meaning and tension. The dramatic content does not derive from large-scale events or major emotional content but from nuances of relationship and misunderstandings: more Jane Austen (had she been a dramatist) than Tolstoy.

There are clearly risks involved in asking a young person to play the part of a foreign visitor, with dangers of stereotyping and superficial mimicry. A considerable amount of 'stage-setting' and workshop activity preceded the final performances which included the following: a game which addressed the issue of stereotyping directly before engaging in the drama; still images; 'living through' interviewing of a teacher in role as a foreign visitor and preparation of monologues (Fleming 1998). By the time the pupils (members of a drama club and hence of mixed ages) worked on their final pieces of devised drama the question of how to represent the foreign visitor was not an issue. As the focus of the drama was on how a visitor can be made to feel alienated in a foreign country, the level of engagement with the content was such that any kind of negative stereotyping became highly unlikely. The situations depicted were fairly ordinary but the pupils built into their work explanations of why the visitors were uncomfortable. They assumed for example that the French visitor would automatically know and care about French footballers. They made no concession in their use of strong north-east accents and dialect. Fish and chips covered with vinegar were provided in newspaper, much to the discomfort of the visitor, with no explanation. They assumed that their visitors would happily watch and understand a soap opera on television. Whether the situations chosen were realistic or not as sources of discomfort was less important than the exploration of how people can unwittingly contribute to the culture shock experienced by visitors. In each case the pupils were 'representing' events from real life. To what degree therefore is 'representation' an adequate account of drama as an aesthetic art form?

Representation

The concept of representation is most clearly related to painting; the simple idea that a picture depicts something that is in the world. This is not dissimilar to Wittgenstein's early account of language and meaning whereby the language 'pictures' or 'mirrors' the real world. The image of a mirror was used by Plato in *The Republic* (p.423) to describe the way in which someone can emulate the skill of the craftsman.

> The quickest way is to take a mirror and turn it round in all directions; before long you will create sun and stars and earth, yourself and all other animals and planets, and furniture and the other objects we mentioned just now.

In Plato's philosophy reality is preferable to appearance and hence the mimetic artist was excluded from the ideal state. Nevertheless the pictorial mimesis 'quickly became the standard account of representation in the Western tradition...and was held more or less as common sense at least through the Renaissance' (Sartwell 1992:365). The 'simple' version of representation assumes a degree of transparency. It does not recognise, as later writers came to believe, that there is no such thing as 'innocent' seeing. It does not take account of the basic Kantian idea that what the artist sees depends on the subjective perspective of the artist; pure imitation is not possible (Gombrich 1960). Another objection (echoing Plato) is that even if simple imitation of the real world is possible, it is not clear what the point is. It is mere duplication. As Veron put it in 1979, 'if the artist were really able to reduce himself to the condition of a copying machine' his work would be a 'servile production' and 'inferior to reality' (quoted in Sartwell 1992:366). Some artists and theorists answered this concern by seeing the process of representation as one of *idealisation*. Art would thus not duplicate the real world but show the way toward a higher plane of reality.

Although accounts of art as representation are usually related to painting (music for example does not appear to be representational in any sense), they can be usefully applied to drama because the parallels are clear. One purpose of drama after all appears to be 'to hold a mirror up to nature'. Representation does seem to offer at least a partial explanation of art. Lyas (1997:38) has pointed out the huge interest in representation in everyday life.

> Interest in representation is as ubiquitous as our involvement with the aesthetic. Pictures are bought in Woolworth's because representation appeals. The waterfront portraitist at Key West trades on a fascination with representation. People seem driven to festoon walls, trains, bridges with representational graffiti. There is an insatiable drive to represent the world, an insatiable wish to view those representations, and a propensity fervently to cherish those gifted as representers. That suggests a central role for representation in any account of the power of art.

It could be argued that what is being referred to here is simply not art. However, the strength of Lyas' account throughout his book is that he is constantly seeking to bridge the gap between so called 'high art' and the bedrock of spontaneous and natural reactions from which art orginates (this was discussed in Chapter 3). It would be a mistake to build a theory of art or of painting which only takes account of highly abstract works and which fails to acknowledge the importance of a simple version of representation. Similarly in the case of drama it would be wrong to deny that one appeal of the art form throughout its history is the way it appears to depict real life. This obvious fact can be forgotten as fashions change. There is if anything now more reference to non-naturalistic conventions in teaching the subject, almost as a reaction to the excessive preoccupation with naturalism which was more dominant in many drama classrooms in the 1970s.

However, it is important to recognise that what often really compels pupils' interest in drama is the degree to which it appears to imitate real life. This is of course particularly true of young children in their dramatic play. Soap operas are very popular with the public, and realistic dramas do engage pupils' interest; it would be a mistake simply to dismiss both as mere manifestation of some sort of low or unsophisticated taste. Pure mimesis or representation, however, is what motivated much of the drama in the 1950s and 1960s and accounts for the vacuity of much of the work at that time. Pupils were asked to imitate actions, act out stories and mimes in order to imitate real life as closely as possible.

Representation then can be seen as a partial but incomplete explanation of art. It needs to be considered alongside the concept of 'expression', which needs further consideration.

Expression

The concept of expression was discussed in Chapter 6 in relation to feeling. The idea that expression is central to understanding in art has its origins in theories of self expression. It was thought that the feelings of the artist are expressed in the work and are then aroused in the spectator who shares the same feelings. This transparent account of the communication of feeling was described in Chapter 6 and the various criticisms summarised.

A more sophisticated theory of art as expression suggests that an artist is someone who gives articulate expression to emotions or feelings in the art work. This is different from the self-expression view because it does away with the idea that the feelings which are expressed by the artist and experienced by the spectator are the same. The artist is propelled by a motivation to 'express' in the sense of 'clarify' feelings by embodying them in artistic form. Different versions of expression theories have been developed by writers like Collingwood, Croce and Langer. According to Collingwood, the distinction between art and craft hinged on the difference between representation and expression. He saw representation as 'a matter of skill, a craft of a special kind' (1938:42). He also distinguished between representation and imitation.

> A work of art is imitative in virtue of its relation to another work of art which affords it a model of artistic excellence; it is representative in virtue of its relation to something in 'nature', that is, something not a work of art.   (ibid: 42)

Expression theory, however, went beyond the concept of representation because it brought a greater sense of passion and emotional conviction in comparison to the craftsman working away methodically and sytematically.

> The expression theory thus incorporated a sharp distinction between the artist, struggling to body forth a specific emotion in all its inchoate uniqueness and so unable to rely upon blueprints or received wisdom, and the craftsman, methodically working towards an independently specifiable product according to tried and tested principles.   (Mulhall 1992:145)

Although different forms of expression theory are more sophisticated than the naive version of self expression they too have been criticised because they are based on the assumption that a feeling exists *prior to* its expression and realisation in the work itself.

Hagberg (1995) has drawn parallels between the problem of creativity in aesthetics and the philosophy of language.

> The creative process in art has often been viewed as a sequence of events through which an inner entity, a particular feeling or emotion, is given external realization.   (ibid:99)

He draws on Wittgenstein's writing on expression and intention to show how the traditional view is misguided. In what Hagberg (1995:101) calls a 'translation' model of art the artistic medium in which an artist is working is given a subordinate role. We are directed by this model to look not at what is on the painter's canvas, or the sculptor's pedestal but through or behind these things to the emotion which the artist is said to be expressing.

In the *Blue and Brown Books* Wittgenstein distinguishes between what he calls transitive and intransitive uses of the words 'peculiar' and 'particular'. The use of the word 'particular' can mislead because two uses can easily become conflated. One is a preliminary to a specification, description or comparison, the other is not.

> The first usage I shall call the transitive one, the second the intransitive. Thus one the one hand I say 'This face gives me a particular impression which I can't describe'. The latter sentence may mean something like: 'This face gives me a strong impression'. These examples would perhaps be more striking if we substituted the word 'peculiar' for 'particular' for the same comments apply to 'peculiar'. If I say, 'This soap has a peculiar smell: it is the kind we used as children', the word 'peculiar' may be used merely as an introduction to the comparison which follows it, as though I said, 'I'll tell you what this soap smells like: . . . .' If, on the other hand, I say 'This soap has a peculiar smell' or 'It has a most peculiar smell', 'peculiar' here stands for some such expression as 'out of the ordinary', 'uncommon', 'striking'.

What relevance do these enigmatic statements have to the concept of expression? When we say that art is a form of expression it is more helpful to see this in terms of an intransitive use, to say that the art form is 'expressive' rather than assuming that the art is expressing a particular emotion. As indicated in Chapter 6, the problem of expression in drama becomes more acute because there are real people having real feelings (of whatever kind) in the course of making the drama. But the intransitive use of the word, that the drama is 'expressive', gets round the problem of having to explain the precise nature of the feelings of the participants. At its most basic the concept of 'expression' is a reminder that art is above all about *human* expression.

Does that mean it is not correct to talk about pupils 'expressing feelings in drama'? It would be entirely against the spirit of the account of language in this book to legislate about particular uses of terms. If language is largely metaphorical then it makes little sense to outlaw forms of linguistic expression. The point is more one to do with practice. If we talk about pupils 'expressing feelings in the drama' and interpret that statement to mean that it is the teacher's role to stir up or evoke particular feelings in advance of the drama then this is where we go wrong. It is then that the deceptive nature of language needs to be uncovered.

The example of a drama about a foreign visitor given at the start of this chapter was deliberately chosen because its content is so ordinary, almost banal. What transforms the drama from being a naive piece of representation is the way in which very ordinary, every day situations are 'defamiliarised' because they are seen through the eyes of an outsider. It is the dramatic art form (the use of monologue to frame the performance and the precise selection of words and movements to convey nuances of meaning) which provides a greater depth of content. The drama embodied or expressed feelings of alienation, frustration, loneliness, confusion. Whether the pupils directly experienced such particular feelings is beside the point. According to Wittgenstein the word 'particular' has little meaning in this context.

Explanations of art have tended to emphasise form, representation or expression. All these concepts, however, are important in describing the way drama functions as an aesthetic art form. Too often the word 'aesthetic' is used in a reductive way to refer just to formal elements of the drama. To narrow it in this way has dire consequences when teaching and assessing the subject as will be illustrated in a discussion of one of Beckett's plays.

Catastrophe

Beckett's play *Catastrophe* is very short, only four pages long. There are four characters: a theatre director, his female assistant, a protagonist and Luke in charge of the lighting (the only one who is given a name). The play consists of a director putting the final touches to the last scene of a play. In keeping with Beckett's minimalist approach we are not told what the play which the director has been working on is about, we just see the final stages of its creation.

Catastrophe was dedicated to Vaclav Havel and was premiered in 1982 during his imprisonment in Czechoslovakia for 'subversion against the state'. It can therefore be seen at one level as a political allegory. The protagonist literally does not speak throughout the play but his presence could be said to 'speak' of someone who has been silenced and subject to forces which have stripped him of his dignity. The protagonist is 'worked on' by the director and assistant in a way which has no respect for his humanity. His gown is taken off to reveal old grey pyjames. Gradually more naked flesh is revealed and the director gives the instruction for it to be whitened. The protagonist is systematically degraded and dehumanised.

However, because we are watching a director at work preparing the ending of a 'play within a play', the piece can also been seen as providing insight into the creative/aesthetic process in making drama. The play is at one level about the creation of aesthetic meaning, for that is precisely what the director and assistant are doing. However, the process in which they are engaged represents a cliché, a form of 'theatricality' (see Chapter 7). The director is dressed in a fur coat and is smoking a cigar. He is the epitome of the dictatorial director (and Beckett may have intended a political parallel) whose actor is there to respond to his directions and ego. The assistant lights the director's cigar and follows his instructions as he experiments with his creation.

D: Light. (A *returns, relights the cigar, stands still.* D *smokes.*)
Good. Now let's have a look. (A *at a loss. Irritably.*) Get going. Lose that gown.
(*He consults his chronometer.*)
Step on it, I have a caucus.
(A *goes to* P, *takes off the gown.* P *submits, inert.* A *steps back, the gown over her arm.* P
in old grey pyjamas head bowed, fist clenched. Pause.)
A: Like him better without? (*Pause.*) He's shivering.
D. Not all that. Hat.
(A *advances, takes off hat, steps back, hat in hand. Pause.*)

The director fulfils the typical stereotype: he is rushed, irritated, rather fickle, a bit
precious, not easily satisfied. As States (1994:202) has pointed out, there is an
idiomatic strain in his language consisting of slang or trade language: 'Step on
it...No harm trying...Bless his heart...Every i dotted to death...Get going!...Is Luke
around...Lovely...Terrific! He'll have them on their feet'. As States puts it, this is
'urban contemporary'. No doubt in an even more contemporary version he would
have been saying 'Cool', 'Brill' or 'Nice one'.

When the assistant timidly suggests that the appearance of the protagonist
might be improved by a little gag the director is scornful.

D: For God's sake! This craze for explication! Every i dotted to death! Little gag.
For God's sake.

Later when she suggests, also very tentatively, that they might lift his head, he is
equally dismissive.

D: For God's sake! What next? Raise his head? Where do you think we are? In
Patagonia? Raise his head? For God's sake! (*Pause.*)

This is amusing satire. The director egotistically assumes that only his own ideas
are of any value; his reaction is far in excess of what was warranted by the tentative
suggestion made by the assistant. However, the exchanges have more significance
than this. What we witness in the 'play within the play' is the act of aesthetic
creation seen as a fairly cynical manipulation of theatrical signs to create effect. It
is all form without content. (We might see in the image of the director a teacher
preparing for the worst kind of GCSE examination.)

As spectators of Beckett's play we are not made aware of the content for the
director's play because we are only seeing the finishing touches to the last dress
rehearsal. But that is why the style and language of the director are so important
because they symbolise the lack of any real concern or genuine expression. At the end
of Beckett's play the director is pleased with what he has created. 'There's our
catastrophe. In the bag' but what he has created is hollow. The play ends with a
distant storm of applause while the protagonist raises his head and fixes the audience.

Given that the author is Beckett we may also see in *Catastrophe* a metaphor for divine creation. On this interpretation the director becomes God and the assistant and Luke are his angels helping him out. The creation of man therefore is viewed in a fairly cynical way and the human condition seen with a combination of a tragic and wry humorous vision. There are no specific lines in the play to reinforce this view. However, themes which appear in the author's other works such as *Waiting for Godot* makes this interpretation of *Catastrophe* more plausible. Lines such as those uttered by Pozzo in *Waiting for Godot* throw light on this particular play.

'They gave birth astride of a grave, the light gleams an instant, then it's night once more.'

This is the vision of life seen in the creation allegory – man is no more than a 'bare, forked, animal' created in a trivial 'aesthetic' way.

The depth of *Catastrophe* lies in the layering of meaning. For the purposes of this chapter the most interesting theme is its depiction of clichéd, hollow theatre-making. But Becket's play (in contrast to the *director's play*) is a celebration of the art form of drama and an insight into some of its depth and mysteries. The protagonist within Beckett's play is endowed with symbolic meaning despite the glib and empty way the director sets about constructing him. His skull is moulting ('a few tufts'); his hands are crippled, 'clawlike'. The play ends with just a light shining on his face. In Becket's play he accrues symbolic significance as a political prisoner or as a symbol of all mankind and evokes our sympathy. States sees in the play 'a critique of theater's own function as a mimetic art' (p.201). There is an ambiguity between the artificial applause which greets the director's play and our own applause for Becket's work. In both cases we have found pleasure in witnessing pain and degradation and our impotence is reinforced. Beckett's play has the kind of depth, complexity and evocation of emotion which belongs to the best drama.

In Chapter 1 a stark contrast was drawn between two types of drama lesson. In the first the teacher had given the pupils a group task to work out how they might represent through dialogue and movement the landing of a spacecraft on an alien planet. In the other lesson, during an improvisation of an imaginary press conference set in the future, four pupils in role as space travellers are being questioned about the civilisation they encountered on another planet. The point was made that it would not be sensible to rush to premature judgement on the basis of one lesson alone. However, if the first lesson is representative of all others then there is reason to worry. These examples were painted very starkly in order to make the point of contrast graphically. However, the more elaborate the form becomes the more the lack of content can be disguised. The form becomes an end in itself, devoid of any real expressive quality. Beckett's play provides us with that insight.

CHAPTER 10

Conclusion

The term 'integration' was adopted in this book not to provide a new theory of teaching drama but to illuminate aspects of theory and practice. It has been more a matter of assembling reminders than suggesting a brand new way of looking at the subject. The view of language underpinning much of the writing makes its aim a matter of 'showing' as much as 'saying'; in other words it is not just a case of arguing rationally and logically for a particular point of view but of demonstrating differences in approaches to the subject by linking the various concepts through common threads. It is hoped that a reasonably composite and consistent picture has emerged, notwithstanding the fact that it is not in the nature of language to do away with 'rough edges'.

One of the questions posed in the Introduction was to ask how the legacy of drama in education practice can be described and interpreted. As Bolton (1998) makes absolutely clear in his history of the subject, Heathcote fundamentally changed the approach to the teaching of drama by placing a major emphasis on meaning and content. The subject was conceived in many different ways before she appeared on the scene: acting out stories, mime, speech exercises, movement, dramatic playing but she began to steer children's drama towards matters of significance. The need for that type of intervention in the history of drama teaching seems strange now. The history of drama itself, when described in terms of the great playwrights, is so clearly about significant issues related to human living that it seems odd to think that so much drama for children was exceedingly trivial.

The concept of 'significant content' was adapted from Bell's theory of form to highlight the importance of this notion. Drama is always about something but that 'something' has to be worth examining and thinking about. That does not mean to suggest that drama must always be about social issues or that it should not explore different forms and styles. It would be a shame, for example, if children did not have the chance to experiment with humour in their drama work. But humour, as we know, is far from being trivial. The concept of 'essential' form links with theories of representation and expression. The starting point for understanding in art and drama is the way in which the fictitious context differs from reality. Human intervention transforms content through use of artistic form. Pure representation is never an adequate explanation of drama practice although this view was implicit in much of the teaching in the 1950s and 1960s.

One of the important ways in which drama functions as an art form is to convey depth and hidden meanings through surface dialogue and actions. As a genre it differs from the novel, an insight which needs to inform practice. It has become common in writing about the teaching of drama to make reference to the 'dramatised society' and present arguments in favour of teaching the subject based on the fact that there is so much drama now on film and television. I think that is a mistake. Study of film and television belongs in media courses. It is important to recognise that 'live' drama is an essential aspect of its power. It is a communal and social activity. The meaning of each unique performance depends on the interaction with an audience. This is a very compelling aspect of its importance in education, particularly at a time when so many young people spend their time in front of screens of one kind or another. It is also an aspect of its significance in relation to language and meaning for the latter occurs in cultural contexts or forms of life. We know people are not flocking to the theatre but that is an argument for strengthening not weakening drama teaching in schools.

One of the major contributions made by drama in education practitioners was the sophisticated pedagogical thinking brought to bear on classroom practice. It is easy to diminish the importance of this as mere 'practice' as opposed to 'theory' (as if theory without practice is of any use or significance). Resolving the tension between 'structure' and 'experience' is one way of describing the important pedagogical insights concealed in what seem to be fairly ordinary classroom techniques and approaches. Not to recognise the central importance of pedagogy is to make the mistake of undervaluing the importance of means.

Many of the concepts discussed in the book are closely associated with forms of dualism which have dogged much of western philosophy. The legacy of drama in education is wrongly thought to reside in particular forms of practice. For some writers this consists in 'living through', spontaneous improvisation with teacher in role. For others it consists in 'process' drama (sometimes confusingly also called 'living through') which uses a wider range of techniques but is also underpinned by the notion that particular types of feeling are associated with particular forms of practice. The problem with this view resides on the surface, in the word 'particular'. Feeling is important in drama. We want pupils to feel animated, committed, engaged, interested, tense, excited, exhilarated and so on. But 'feeling engagement' is not confined to one set of practices or one type of activity.

It may seem ironic in a book which contains some fairly hefty chunks of theory to say that in drama teaching there has been a tendency to over-theorise but that is precisely what has happened. We have been digging too deep, looking behind the surface actions to account for the quality of experience of participants in the drama.

We have been looking at 'inner experiences' associated with notions like 'feeling' and 'intention' instead of looking on the surface. However, to say that we should be simply looking on the surface is also potentially misleading. 'Looking on the surface' must mean also looking at the context. We have to look outwards and horizontally rather than inwards. That is when the important notion of 'quality of experience' starts to make sense.

This emphasis on context provides a perspective on the place of performance in drama. There has been a gradual realisation over the years that an audience is an important element in all drama because even in a whole-group spontaneous improvisation without a traditional audience, the participants have a sense of audience or form an audience for their own and others' work. There has been a reluctance however to acknowledge for fear of promoting the wrong kinds of superficial work that in the same way all drama is about performance. But the solution here is again much more on the surface than has been realised. We can distinguish between good and bad, appropriate and inappropriate performances. The importance of looking 'horizontally' is to recognise that in an educational context process is extremely important. Assessment of drama is likely to be limited in scope if it only looks at pupils' performance without any sense of the context in which the work arose.

Many of the early writers on drama showed considerable wisdom when they warned about the dangers of putting young children 'on the stage'. Their notion of performance was of course fairly narrow and their concept of what preparing for a performance should be like inevitably very traditional. However, their insights have considerable relevance. But it is more a matter of sensitivity, judgement and good teaching to know what the right course of action is instead of trying to establish differences in types of performance based on theoretical perspectives. It is fairly common sense to suggest that when preparing for a major public performance as opposed to presenting drama in a workshop some priorities will change. The recommendation that the commonly accepted three attainment targets should be reduced to two (making and responding) was not intended to denigrate performance. On the contrary it elevates its central place in drama. Similarly responding to drama needs to be seen not as a bolt on extra but an integral part of the teaching process.

The view of language which has underpinned this book suggests that script should have a more prominent place in drama lessons than has often been the case. We need to distinguish between speech and writing in ways which seem at first to run counter to common sense. Although meaning in the spoken words feels 'present' and 'immediate' it is often by working on script that pupils can gain greater insight into the way language works and has meaning.

Two views of language derived from Wittgenstein can be extended to embrace many of the other concepts which have been discussed in this book. An exclusive, or at least exaggerated, focus on logic, structure and form leads to the fixity of dead convention. The human dimension is marginalised in favour of the attraction of order and stability. Drama teaching takes place in an educational context in which discussion about values and ends has given way to an obsession with efficiency, objectives and targets. Drama teaching does not sit easily within orderly schemes of progression and assessment but neither can it exist outside the prevailing norms and expectations in education.

Drama in education practice brought a strong element of Dionysian animation, surging energy, creativity and significance onto the drama teaching scene. Mistakes were made; boundaries were exceeded. But the alternative approach is to risk a form of complacent certainty which derives from the tyranny of form over content, structure over experience and logic over meaning.

References

Abbs, P. (1992) 'Abbs replies to Bolton', *Drama* 1(1), 2–6.

Ackroyd, J. (1995) 'But tell me where do the children play? A response to Helen Nicholson', *Drama: The Journal of National Drama* 3(2), 2–6.

Ackroyd, J. (2000) *Literacy Alive*. London: Hodder and Stoughton.

Allen, J. (1979) *Drama in Schools: Its Theory and Practice*. London: Heinemann.

Arts Council of Great Britain (1992) *Drama in Schools*. London: Arts Council.

Atkinson, T. and Claxton, G. (eds) (2000) *The Intuitive Practitioner*. Buckingham: Open University Press.

Barlow, S. and Skidmore, S. (1994) *Dramaform – A Practical Guide to Drama Techniques*. London: Hodder and Stoughton.

Bell, C. (1969) 'Significant form', in Hospers, J. (ed.) (1969) *Introductory Readings in Aesthetics*. London: The Free Press Collier-Macmillan.

Bennathan, J. (2000) *Developing Drama Skills*. London: Heinemann.

Bennett, S. (1997) *Theatre Audiences – A Theory of Production and Reception*. London: Routledge.

Berry, C. (1993) *The Actor and the Text*. London: Virgin Books. (First published in 1987 as *The Actor and His Text* by Harrap.)

Blake, N. *et al.* (1998) *Thinking Again: Education After Postmodernism*. London: Bergin and Garvey.

Blake, N. *et al.* (2000) *Education in an Age of Nihilism*. London: Routledge.

Bolton, G. (1979) *Towards a Theory of Drama in Education*. London: Longman.

Bolton, G. (1981) 'Drama in education: a reappraisal', in Davis, D. and Lawrence, C. (eds) *Gavin Bolton: Selected Writings*. London: Longman.

Bolton, G. (1984) *Drama as Education*. London: Longman.

Bolton, G. (1998) *Acting in Classroom Drama*. Stoke-on-Trent: Trentham Books.

Bolton, G. (1999) 'Review of *Beginning Drama 11–14* by Neelands, J.', in *Drama: The Journal of National Drama* 7(1), 41.

Bolton, G. and Heathcote, D. (1999) *So You Want to Use Role-Play? A New Approach in How to Plan*. Stoke-on-Trent: Trentham Books.

Bowell, P. and Heap, B. S. (2001) *Planning Process Drama*. London: David Fulton Publishers.

Bowie, A. (1990) *Aesthetics and Subjectivity from Kant to Nietzsche*. Manchester: Manchester University Press.

Brecht, B. (1947) *Galileo*. English version by Charles Laughton. Indiana: Indiana University Press.

Broadfoot, P. (2000) 'Assessment and intuition', in Atkinson, T. and Claxton, G. (eds) *The Intuitive Practitioner*. Buckingham: Open University Press.

Byron, K. (1987) 'Progression in Drama', *2D*, 7, 53–80.

Carr, D. (ed.) *Education, Knowledge and Truth*. London: Routledge.

Central Advisory Council for Education (England) (CACE) (1967) *Children and their Primary Schools* (The Plowden Report). London: HMSO.

Chaplin, A. (1999) *Drama 9–11.* Leamington Spa: Scholastic.

Clark, J. and Goode, T. (1999) (eds) *Assessing Drama.* London: National Drama Publications.

Clark, A. and Short, P. (1999) 'Process or performance', in *Drama: The Journal of National Drama* 7(1), 7–11.

Collingwood, R. (1938) *The Principles of Art.* Oxford: Clarendon Press.

Collinson, D. (1992) 'Aesthetic experience', in Hanfling, O. *Philosophical Aesthetics: An Introduction.* Oxford: Blackwell.

Cooper, D. (1990) *Existentialism – A Reconstruction.* Oxford: Blackwell.

Cooper, D. (ed.) (1992) *A Companion to Aesthetics.* Oxford: Blackwell.

Cooper, D. (1998) 'The postmodern ethos', in Carr, D. (ed.) *Education, Knowledge and Truth.* London: Routledge.

Courtney, R. (1968) *Play, Drama and Thought: The Intellectual Background to Drama in Education.* London: Cassell.

Cox, B. (1989) *English for Ages 5–16.* (The Cox Report). London: HMSO (published by the DES).

Cox, B. (1991) *Cox on Cox: An English Curriculum for the 1990s.* London: Hodder and Stoughton.

Croce, B. (1992) *The Aesthetic of Science of Expression and of the Linguistic in General.* Translated by Colin Lyas. Cambridge: Cambridge University Press.

Daldry, S. (1998) 'Foreword', in Hornbrook, D. (ed.) *On the subject of Drama.* London: Routledge.

Davies, G. (1985) 'Let's avoid stirring up old conflicts', *Drama Broadsheet* 2(3), 1.

Davis, D. (1985) 'Dorothy Heathcote interviewed by David Davis', *2D*, 4(3), 64–80.

Davis, D. and Lawrence, C. (1986) *Gavin Bolton: Selected Writings.* London: Longman.

Deane, S. (1996) 'Introduction', in *Brian Friel: Plays.* London: Faber and Faber.

Derrida, J. (1978) *Writing and Difference.* Chicago: University of Chicago Press.

DES (1989) *English for Ages 5–16.* (The Cox Report). London: HMSO.

Dewey, J. (1934) *Art as Experience.* New York: Capricorn (1958 edn).

Dewey, J. (1938) *Experience and Education.* London: Collier Macmillan.

DfEE (1998) *The National Literacy Strategy.* London: DfEE.

Doll, W. (1993) *A Postmodern Perspective on Curriculum.* New York: Teachers' College Press.

Donaldson, M. (1978) *Children's Minds.* London: Fontana.

Eagleton, T. (1987) *Saints and Scholars.* London: Verso.

Eaton, M. (1988) *Basic Issues in Aesthetics.* California: Wadsworth.

Elam, K. (1988) *The Semiotics of Theatre and Drama.* London: Routledge.

Eldridge, R. (1992) 'Form', in Cooper, D. (ed.) *A Companion to Aesthetics.* Oxford: Blackwell.

Esslin, M. (1987) *The Field of Drama.* London: Methuen.

Finch, H. L. (1995) *Wittgenstein.* Dorset: Element Books.

Fleming, M. (1985) 'Teaching and expression', *Drama Broadsheet* 3(3), 8–9.

Fleming, M. (1994) *Starting Drama Teaching.* London: David Fulton Publishers.

Fleming, M. (1997a) 'Teacher-in-role revisited', *The Secondary English Magazine* 1(1), 20–2.

Fleming, M. (1997b) *The Art of Drama Teaching.* London: David Fulton Publishers.

Fleming, M. (1998) 'Cultural awareness and dramatic art forms', in Byram, M. and Fleming, M. (eds) *Language Learning in Intercultural Perspective.* Cambridge: Cambridge University Press.

Fleming, M. (1999a) 'Poetry and Drama: not waving but drowning', *The Secondary English Magazine* 2(4), 22–5.

Fleming, M. (1999b) 'Progression and continuity in the teaching of Drama', *Drama: The Journal of National Drama* 7(1), 12–18.

Fleming, M. (1999c) 'An integrated approach to drama for aesthetic learning', *NJ (Drama Australia Journal)* 23(2), 91–9.

Fleming, M. (2000) 'A highwayman comes riding', in Ackroyd, J. *Literacy Alive*. London: Hodder and Stoughton.

Fleming, M. (2001) 'What do we mean by teaching drama', in Williamson, J. *et al. Meeting the Standards in Secondary English*. London: Routledge/Falmer.

Genova, J. (1995) *Wittgenstein A Way of Seeing*. London: Routledge.

Gibson, R. (1998) *Teaching Shakespeare*. Cambridge: Cambridge University Press.

Glock, H. (1996) *A Wittgenstein Dictionary*. Oxford: Blackwell.

Gombrich, E. (1960) *Art and Illusion: A Study in the Psychology of Pictorial Representation*. Oxford: Phaidon.

Goodridge, J. (1970) *Drama in the Primary School*. London: Heinemann.

Goodwyn, A. (1992) 'English teachers and the Cox models', *English in Education* 28(3), 4–10.

Graham, G. (1997) *Philosophy of the Arts*. London: Routledge.

Grayling, A. (1996) *Wittgenstein*. Oxford: Oxford University Press. (First published in 1988 by Oxford University Press.)

Greger, S. (1969) 'Presentational theories need unpacking', *The British Journal of Aesthetics* 9(2), 157–70.

Hagberg, G. (1995) *Art As Language: Wittgenstein, Meaning and Aesthetic Theory*. Ithaca: Cornell University Press.

Hahlo, R. and Reynolds, P. (2000) *Dramatic Events: How to Run a Successful Workshop*. London: Faber.

Handke, P. (1997) *Plays*. London: Methuen.

Hanfling, O. (ed.) (1992) *Philosophical Aesthetics: An Introduction*. Oxford: Blackwell.

Hardman, F. (2001) 'What do we mean by media education in English?', in Williamson, J. *et al.* (2001) *Meeting the Standards in Secondary English*. London: Falmer Press.

Hardman, F. and Williamson, J. (1993) 'Student teachers and models of English', *Journal of Education for Teaching* 19, 279–92.

Harland, J. *et al.* (2000) *Arts Education in Secondary Schools: Effects and Effectiveness*. Windsor: NFER.

Hawkes, T. (1991) *Structuralism and Semiotics*. London: Routledge. (First published in 1977 by Methuen.)

Hirst, P. (1974) *Knowledge and the Curriculum*. London: Routledge.

Hornbrook, D. (1989) *Education and Dramatic Art*. London: Blackwell Education.

Hornbrook, D. (1991) *Education in Drama: Casting the Dramatic Curriculum*. London: Falmer Press.

Hornbrook, D. (ed.) (1998) *On The Subject of Drama*. London: Routledge.

Hospers, J. (ed.) (1969) *Introductory Readings in Aesthetics*. London: The Free Press Collier-Macmillan.

Hughes, R. (1993) 'Tolstoy, Stanislavski, and the Art of Acting', *The Journal of Aesthetics and Art Criticism* 51(1), 38–48.

Irwin, S. (2000) 'Physical theatre', in Nicholson, H. (ed.) *Teaching Drama 11–18*. London: Continuum.

James, W. (1977) *Pragmatism in The Writings of William James*. Chicago: University of Chicago Press.

Johnson, L. and O'Neill, C. (1984) *Dorothy Heathcote: Selected Writings on Education and Drama*. London: Hutchinson.

Kaelin, E. F. (1989) *An Aesthetics for Art Educators*. New York: Teachers' College Press.

Kempe, A. and Ashwell, M. (2000) *Progression in Secondary Drama*. London: Heinemann.

Kempe, A. and Warner, L. (1997) *Starting With Scripts*. Cheltenham: Stanley Thornes.

Kuhn, T. (1997) 'Introduction', in Handke, P. *Plays 1*. London: Methuen.

Langer, S. (1953) *Feeling and Form*. London: Routledge and Kegan Paul.

Lewicki, T. (1996) *From 'Play Way' to 'Dramatic Art'*. Rome: Libreria Ateneo Salesiano.

Lodge, D. (ed.) (1988) *Modern Criticism and Theory*. London: Longman.

Lyas, C. (1973) 'Personal qualities and The Intentional Fallacy', in Vesey, G. (ed.) *Philosophy and the Arts*. London: Macmillan.

Lyas, C. (1997) *Aesthetics*. London: UCL Press.

McGinn, M. (1997) *Wittgenstein and The Philosophical Investigations*. London: Routledge.

Monk, R. (1991) *Ludwig Wittgenstein: The Duty of Genius*. London: Vintage (first published in 1990 by Jonathan Cape).

Morgan, N. and Saxton, J. (1987) *Teaching Drama*. London: Hutchinson.

Mulhall, S. (1992) 'Expression', in Cooper, D. (ed.) (1992) *A Companion to Aesthetics*. Oxford: Blackwell.

National Drama Association (1998) *The National Drama Secondary Drama Teacher's Handbook*. London: National Drama Publications.

NCC (1990) *The Arts 5–16: A Curriculum Framework*. London: Oliver and Boyd.

Neelands, J. (1998) *Beginning Drama 11–14*. London: David Fulton Publishers.

Neelands, J. (2000) 'Drama sets you free – or does it', in Davison, J. and Moss, J. *Issues in English Teaching*. London: Routledge.

Neelands, J. and Dobson, W. (2000) *Drama and Theatre Studies at AS/A Level*. London: Hodder and Stoughton.

Nietzsche, F. (1968) *The Will to Power*. New York: Vintage Books.

Neitzsche, F. (2000) *The Birth of Tragedy*. Oxford: Oxford University Press. (First published in 1872.)

Nicholson, H. (1994) 'Drama and the Arts: from polemic to practice', *Drama: The Journal of National Drama* 3(1), 2–23.

Nicholson, H. (ed.) (2000) *Teaching Drama 11–18*. London: Continuum.

Norman, J. (1999) 'Brain right drama', *Drama: The Journal of National Drama* 6(2), 8–13.

Norris, C. (1982) *Deconstruction Theory and Practice*. London: Methuen. (Revised edition published in 1991 by Routledge.)

O'Neill, C. (1995) *Drama Worlds*. New Hampshire: Heinemann.

O'Neill, C. and Lambert, A. (1982) *Drama Structures: A Practical Handbook for Teachers*. London: Hutchinson.

O'Toole, J. (1992) *The Process of Drama Negotiating Art and Meaning*. London: Routledge.

Owens, A. and Barber, K. (1997) *Dramaworks*. Carlisle: Carel Press.

Pavis, P. (1992) *Theatre at the Crossroads of Culture*. London and New York: Routledge.

Pavis, P. (ed.) (1996) *The Intercultural Performance Reader*. London: Routledge.

Pemberton-Billing, R. and and Clegg, J. (1965) *Teaching Drama*. London: University of London Press.

Peter, M. (1994) *Drama For All*. London: David Fulton Publishers.

Peters, M. and Marshall, J. (1999) *Wittgenstein: Philosophy, Postmodernism, Pedagogy*. London: Bergin and Garvey.

Peters, R. S. (ed.) (1969) *Perspectives on Plowden*. London: Routledge.

Pine, R. (1990) *Brian Friel and Ireland's Drama*. London: Routledge.

Pinker, S. (1994) *The Language Instinct*. London: Penguin.

Plato (1955) *The Republic*. Translated by Desmond Lee. Harmonworth: Penguin.

Robinson, K. (1980) *Exploring Theatre and Education*. London: Heinemann.

Roose-Evans, J. (1968) *Directing a Play*. London: Studio Vista.

Rorty, R. (1989) *Contingency, Irony and Solidarity*. Cambridge: Cambridge University Press.

Sartre, J. (1972) *The Psychology of Imagination*. London: Methuen. (First published in France in 1940 with the title *L'Imaginaire*.)

Sartwell, C. (1992) 'Representation', in Cooper, D. (ed.) *A Companion to Aesthetics*. Oxford: Blackwell.

Schechner, R. (1988) *Performance Theory*. London: Routledge.

Secondary Heads Association (SHA) (1998) *Drama Sets you Free!* Leicester: SHA.

Seely, J. (1976) *In Context: Language and Drama in the Secondary School*. Oxford: Oxford University Press.

Shklovsky, V. (1988) 'Art as technique', in Lodge, D. (ed.) *Modern Criticism and Theory*. London: Longman. (First published in 1965 in *Russian Formalist Criticism*.)

Sim, S. (1992) 'Structuralism and poststructuralism', in Hanfling, O. (ed.) *Philosophical Aesthetics.* Oxford: Blackwell.

Simons, J. (2000) 'Walking in another person's shows: storytelling and role-play', in Nicholson, H. (ed.) *Teaching Drama 11–18.* London: Continuum.

Slade, P. (1954) *Child Drama.* London: University of London Press.

Sluga, A. and Stern, D. (eds) (1996) *The Cambridge Companion to Wittgenstein.* Cambridge: Cambridge University Press.

Smeyers, P. and Marshall, D. (eds) (1995) *Philosophy and Education: Accepting Wittgenstein's Challenge.* Dordrecht: Kluwer Academic Publishers.

Smith, D. (2000) 'Introduction', in Neitzsche, F. *The Birth of Tragedy.* Oxford: Oxford University Press.

Sokal, A. and Bricmont, J. (1998) *Intellectual Impostures: Postmodern philosophers' abuse of science.* London Profile Books (first published in French in 1997).

Somers, J. (1994) *Drama in the Curriculum.* London: Cassell.

Staten, H. (1986) *Wittgenstein and Derrida.* Nebraska: University of Nebraska Press.

States, B. (1985) *Great Reckonings in Little Rooms: On the Phenomenology of Theater.* California: University of California Press.

States, B. (1994) *The Pleasures of the Play.* Ithaca: Cornell University Press.

Stobart, G. and Gipps, C. (1990) *Assessment: A Teacher's Guide to the Issues.* London: Hodder and Stoughton.

Styan, J. (1981) *Modern Drama in Theory and Practice 2. Symbolism, Surrealism and the Absurd.* Cambridge: Cambridge University Press.

Szondi, P. (1987) *Theory of the Modern Drama.* Cambridge: Polity Press.

Taylor, P. (2000) *The Drama Classroom: Action, Reflection, Transformation.* London: Routledge/Falmer.

Tolstoy, L. (1996, first published 1896) *What is Art?* Translated by Aylmer Maude. Indiana: Hackett Publishing.

Tormey, A. (1971) *The Concept of Expression.* Princeton: Princeton University Press.

Tully, J. (ed.) (1994) *Philosophy in an Age of Pluralism.* Cambridge: Cambridge University Press.

Urian, D. (1998) 'On being an audience: a spectactor's guide', in Hornbrook, D. (ed.) *On the Subject of Drama.* London: Routledge.

Wagner, B. (1976) *Drama as a Learning Medium.* Washington: National Education Association.

Wallis, M. and Shepherd, S. (1998) *Studying Plays.* London: Arnold.

Way, B. (1967) *Development Through Drama.* London: Longman.

Wilkinson, R. (1992) 'Art, emotion and expression', in Hanfling, O. (ed.) *Philosophical Aesthetics: An Introduction.* Oxford: Blackwell.

Williamson, J. *et al.* (2001) *Meeting the Standards in Secondary English.* London: Routledge/Falmer.

Winston, J. (1998) *Drama, Narrative and Moral Education.* London: Falmer Press.

Winston, J. (2000) *Drama, Literacy and Moral Education 5–11.* London: David Fulton Publishers.

Winston, J. and Tandy, M. (1998) *Beginning Drama 4–11.* London: David Fulton Publishers. (2nd edn 2001.)

Wittgenstein, L. (1953) *Philosophical Investigations.* Oxford: Blackwell.

Wittgenstein, L. (1958) *The Blue and Brown Books.* Oxford: Blackwell.

Wittgenstein, L. (1961) *Tractatus Logico Philosophicus.* Translated by C. K. Ogden and F. P. Ramsey. London: Routledge and Kegan Paul. (First published in 1922.)

Wittgenstein, L. (1969) *On Certainty.* Oxford: Blackwell.

Wittgenstein, L. (1998) *Culture and Value.* Oxford: Blackwell.

Woolland, B. (1993) *The Teaching of Drama in the Primary School.* London: Longman.

Young, J. (1992) 'Neitzshe', in Cooper, D. (ed.) *A Companion to Aesthetics.* Oxford: Blackwell.

Index